Echoes of Life

A Journey of Self-discovery and Inner Transformation

DR AJAYPAL KALYAN

An imprint of
Srishti Publishers & Distributors

Srishti Publishers & Distributors
A unit of AJR Publishing LLP
212A, Peacock Lane
Shahpur Jat, New Delhi – 110 049

editorial@srishtipublishers.com

First published by Bold,
an imprint of Srishti Publishers & Distributors in 2024

10 9 8 7 6 5 4 3 2 1

This is a work of non-fiction, based on the authors' experiences and life-learnings. It provides practical solutions to everyday problems, but the recommendations given herein are in no way intended to be a substitute for professional advice and help.

Printed and bound in India.

For my Parents

&

Readers who want to transform their life…

CONTENTS

PREFACE

Who are you?

Why are you here in this world? What is your purpose?

Does it matter to anyone if your part in their life suddenly gets erased?

There are so many questions and the answers lie in the pages of books.

As a bibliophile and a seeker of life's deeper truths, I've always found solace and inspiration in the pages of books. Through the diverse narratives of well-known personalities and perspectives from different walks of life, I've embarked on countless journeys of introspection and self-discovery, pondering the true potential of the human brain and what stops it from achieving the unachievable.

Over the years, I've immersed myself in a variety of experiences, from exploring remote landscapes to engaging in meaningful conversations with individuals from various fields. Through these encounters, I've come to realize the profound impact that authentic connections and relationships have on personal growth and fulfillment.

This book is the culmination of my reflections and insights from a lifetime of exploration and contemplation. Each chapter delves into a different facet of the human experience, from navigating the complexities of modern-day connectivity to harnessing the power of the unconscious mind.

In these pages, you'll find reflections on the tension between progress and justice, the battle between ego and unconsciousness, and the importance of cultivating gratitude and resilience in the face of life's uncertainties. Drawing upon my own experiences and observations, I aim to provide readers with practical tools and insights to navigate life's curveballs with grace and resilience.

Ultimately, this book is a testament to the power of introspection and self-awareness in unlocking our true potential and living a life of purpose and meaning. I hope that it serves as a source of inspiration and guidance for readers on their own journeys of self-discovery and personal growth.

So, dear reader, I invite you to explore these pages with an open mind and an adventurous spirit. Have faith and let's take a leap into the world of books and experiences.

ACKNOWLEDGMENTS

This book's writing process has been just as transformative as the exploration it encourages. I'm profoundly thankful to the innumerable people who have added to its creation, straightforwardly or in a roundabout way.

To my loved ones, whose faithful help and confidence in me have been an anchor in the meantime. Your support and patience have been extremely helpful.

I'd like to express my sincere gratitude to the thinkers, writers, and artists whose works have helped me better understand the world. The concepts presented in this book are the result of their insights.

To the readers, whose enquiring minds and willingness to hear new points of view make this endeavor worthwhile. The final indicator of this book's impact will be your engagement with these ideas.

Last but not least, I acknowledge the significant impact that my positive and negative life experiences have had on my perspective and laid the groundwork for this investigation. I sincerely hope that you will find this book to be a helpful guide on your own personal growth and self-discovery journey.

1

EXPLORE YOUR POTENTIAL AND ASK YOURSELF, HOW FAR CAN YOU GO?

Because of the way we were built, we humans can never settle on a single accomplishment. The fact that we are always striving to improve ourselves and reach new heights, horizons, and accomplish things is what sets us apart from all the other beings that inhabit this world. But then, the question that keeps coming up in some form or another is, what exactly is the point of our existence here on Earth? Are we simply here to have fun, discover new things, and develop our potential? And if we reached the limit, then what would be the next step? What are we doing this for? Who exactly are we?

One quote that speaks to the challenge of finding answers to deep questions comes from the philosopher Friedrich Nietzsche, who said: ***"The problem with looking for truth is that you invariably find it."*** Nietzsche recognized that our search for truth is often fraught with difficulties, as the answers we uncover may challenge our existing beliefs and force us to confront uncomfortable realities.

Similarly, the philosopher Immanuel Kant wrote: ***"Out of the crooked timber of humanity, no straight thing was ever made."*** This quote speaks to the idea that human nature is inherently flawed and imperfect, which can make it difficult to find straightforward answers to complex questions. Our biases, limitations, and contradictions can make it challenging to arrive at definitive answers to many of life's big questions.

Despite these challenges, there are many other quotes that emphasize the importance of continuing to search for answers, even when the path ahead may be difficult. For example, the physicist Albert Einstein once said: ***"The important thing is not to stop questioning. Curiosity has its own reason for existing."***

Similarly, the writer and philosopher Voltaire once said: ***"Judge a man by his questions rather than by his answers."*** By asking thoughtful questions and engaging in intellectual exploration, we can deepen our understanding of the world and gain valuable insights into the nature of truth, knowledge, and reality.

Even with the power of recorded testaments and the books written by visionaries and various men of wisdom, it is difficult to find answers to the questions that have been posed above. This is because deciphering the texts and logic presented by them is the most difficult task for our generation because we have progressed from that state and are now the newer version of ourselves. However, it is important to continue seeking answers and exploring our purpose as individuals and as a society. Through introspection, education, and collaboration, we can better understand who we are and what we are working towards. But then there are restrictions for us. The restrictions are in terms of time and 'memory.' The concept of time is easy to understand, but let me brief you on the concept of memory.

"Memory is the diary that we all carry about with us."

– Oscar Wilde

Our genes are the fundamental component of everything about our physical selves that we can legitimately claim as our own. All the things that have been with us since the day we were born on this planet are the direct or indirect results of our genetics, which holds true even for all other species. Our personalities, our quirks, and even our memories are all products of our hereditary makeup. Genetic coding has been passed down from generation to generation, which includes not only physical traits but also behavioural tendencies. The 'memory' of our ancestors is embedded in our DNA, and that gets revealed slowly to us as we progress in our lives. Socrates believed that all knowledge is innate and that we simply need to uncover it through questioning and reflection. Therefore, it is possible that a young child's understanding of appropriate behaviour is not solely learned through observation and experience, but also inherited through their genetic makeup. We refer to learning as the process of peeling back the layers of our understanding that contain information that we already possess. Because of this, the animals continue to behave in the same predictable pattern. When hungry, sheep will continue to stick with their flocks, while lizards will continue to consume their young.

In the world of animals, everything is governed by a set of rules; however, in comparison to other animals, humans are regarded as the superior species. This is because we can recognize patterns and decipher things that are unethical in our society. We can tell the difference between what is bad and what is good. This capability can be directly attributed to our emotional intelligence, which is also influenced by our genetics. This emotional intelligence has allowed us to create complex social structures, develop advanced technologies, and build civilizations. However, it also comes with the responsibility to use our intelligence and power for the betterment of all living beings on this planet. Because of this characteristic, we began to behave as though we were the saviors of other species on the planet. However, in doing so, we forgot that many of these species had been coexisting peacefully on this planet long before we ever appeared here. We messed with their natural form, and in our pursuit of harmony in the natural world, we forgot about our place in society. Now, as a result of our complicated nature and the complicated relationships we have with one another as a species, we are unsure of what we are supposed to be doing here. We need to re-evaluate our role in the natural world and strive to coexist peacefully with other species rather than imposing our own ideas on what is best for them. It's time to recognize that we are just one small part of a much larger ecosystem.

Because the religious writings we adhere to are also a source of our understanding of what is right and what is wrong, I believe that even our religion defines who we are and how we perceive the world around us. Because of this, it is important to not only rethink how we relate to the natural world but also to look closely at the cultural and social norms that shape how we see our place in it. This is because these norms have a lot to do with how we see our place in the natural world. It changes what we believe, and what we believe is the basis for how we understand the world. Because the stories and religious texts that we read and follow become our source for determining what is wrong and what is right, it is nearly impossible to rule out the possibility that we become what we hear and where we live.

Hence, if everything operates according to a predetermined set of laws, and all we are doing is acting according to a predetermined set of social norms, how can we possibly get to the bottom of the question that raises the most fundamental question about our existence? How are we going to communicate with our internal selves?

The first answer to the above question could be, "*In order to communicate with our internal selves, we need to critically examine the stories and religious texts that we read and follow and question the social norms that dictate our behaviour. Only then can we begin to understand and connect with our true selves.*" Or, the second one would be to forget everything and start over. The first approach involves a critical analysis of our beliefs and norms, while the second approach suggests a complete abandonment of them. Both approaches aim to help us connect with our true selves and find answers to the most fundamental questions about our existence. It is best to experience things for ourselves if we want to know who we are on the inside. Isn't it true that experiencing an area firsthand is always preferable to looking at a picture of it or watching a movie that was filmed there? It is necessary for us to get out there, talk to a variety of individuals, and have a comprehensive understanding of everything; nevertheless, there is another component involved, and that is time. We are not provided with a sufficient amount of time to experience everything that we want and then reflect on those experiences.

Does this imply that we can never have a complete understanding of who we are? Not necessarily. While we may not experience everything, we can prioritise what is most important to us and attempt to seek out those experiences. Through introspection and reflection on our experiences, we can continue to learn and grow in our understanding of ourselves.

LETTING GO OF YOUR FEARS

"I learned that courage was not the absence of fear, but the triumph over it. The brave man is not he who does not feel afraid, but he who conquers that fear." Nelson Mandela's words echo Mark Twain's sentiment when he said, *"Courage is resistance to fear, mastery of fear, not absence of fear"*. Both of them emphasize that true courage comes from overcoming our fears, not from being free of them. We can all find the strength to face our fears and move forward, even when we feel afraid.

Getting to know yourself begins with overcoming your fear. The first thing holding us back from exploring the uncharted and going down the path less travelled is our natural aversion to the unknown. Let's understand the concept by following the story of Sam.

Exams are a stressful time for many students, and the fear of failure can be overwhelming. This was the case for Sam, a young boy who was always nervous about his exams. As the day of the test got closer, Sam's anxiety grew, and he started to worry too much about the results.

He had studied hard and revised all the lessons, but he couldn't shake off the fear of failure. Sam's mind was filled with thoughts of not being able to do well in the exams, which made it difficult for him to focus on his studies. The pressure of performing well was becoming too much for him to bear.

On the day of the exam, Sam sat nervously at his desk, his heart beating fast. He had worked hard and was well-prepared, but his fear of failing kept getting in the way of his judgment. He felt like he could never do well in the exams, and this made it challenging for him to concentrate.

However, when the results were announced, Sam was surprised to see that he had done very well. In fact, he had scored better than he had expected. This realization made him understand that he had been fearing the results instead of focusing on his hard work before the exam.

This is a common problem among students whose fear of failing can get so big that it gets in the way of their work. A mind is a powerful tool, and it can either be our greatest ally or our worst enemy. When we focus on our fears, we are giving them more power than they deserve.

To truly know ourselves, we must step outside of our comfort zones and explore the road less travelled. This road can be scary, unknown, and filled with uncertainties, but it is essential for our personal growth and self-discovery. We may worry about failure, judgment from others, or even the possibility of discovering something about ourselves that we do not like. But it is precisely these fears that we need to overcome to truly know ourselves.

> ***"The road less travelled is sometimes fraught with barricades, bumps, and uncharted terrain. But it is on that road where your character is truly tested - and your personal growth realized."***
>
> – Christine E. Ray

The road less travelled may be difficult, but it is often the path that leads to the most growth and self-discovery.

It allows us to break free from our comfort zones and challenge ourselves to become better versions of ourselves. By embracing the road less travelled, we can also gain a new perspective on life. We may find that our passions and interests lie in unexpected places and that our true calling in life is something we had never considered before.

FOCUS ON WHAT YOU ARE MOST INTERESTED IN, WORK HARD TO ACHIEVE IT, AND THEN SEE WHERE IT LEADS

Our innate interests and inclinations frequently shape the unique journey that is the pursuit of a hobby. While we may have some control over the hobbies we pursue, it is often the case that our hobbies choose us, rather than the other way around.

Most of the time, we become interested in a certain hobby because we naturally want to do it and are passionate about it. In fact, a hobby is all about giving us a way to express ourselves, be creative, and feel satisfied with ourselves. It is a means of channeling our energy and enthusiasm into something that we are deeply passionate about, and in doing so, we find a sense of purpose and meaning in our lives.

Finding a hobby that speaks to us can be an exciting and life-changing process. It requires us to be open to new things, trust our guts, and give ourselves the freedom to explore without any expectations or ideas we already have.

"A hobby is a defiance of the contemporary. It is an assertion of those permanent values which the momentary eddies of social evolution have contravened or overlooked," as Grace Paley suggests. By pursuing hobbies that speak to us, we can stay connected to our passions and values, even as the world around us changes.

While we may not always be conscious of it, our hobbies can also reveal a great deal about our personalities, interests, and values. They can serve as a reflection of our unique identities and help us understand ourselves better.

One example of a famous personality whose hobbies reveal a lot about their personality and values is former US President Barack Obama.

Obama is known for his love of reading, which he has said helped him to develop empathy and understanding for others. He has cited works of literature such as Ralph Ellison's "Invisible Man" and Toni Morrison's "Song of Solomon" as being particularly influential in his worldview.

Besides reading, Obama is also known for his love of basketball, which he played regularly during his time in office. This hobby reflects his competitive nature and his love of teamwork and collaboration.

Finally, Obama is also a skilled writer and has authored several books, including his memoir "Dreams from My Father." This hobby reflects his passion for storytelling and his belief in the power of language to inspire change and bring people together.

Taken together, Obama's hobbies reveal a complex and multifaceted personality, characterized by empathy, competitiveness, and a commitment to storytelling and language. His hobbies also reflect his values, such as teamwork, collaboration, and a belief in the power of literature to foster understanding and promote social change.

Another such example lies in the story of Bob Marley. Marley was passionate about music and used it as a platform to spread messages of love, peace, and social justice. His music was influenced by his Jamaican roots and the struggles he saw in his community, and it often reflected his commitment to fighting for equality and freedom.

Besides music, Marley was also an avid soccer player and fan. He saw the sport as a way to bring people together and break down barriers between different communities. He once said, ***"Football is a whole skill in itself. A whole world. A whole universe to itself. I love it because you have to be skillful to play it!"***

Finally, Marley was also a practitioner of Rastafarianism, a religion that emphasizes the importance of spiritual and moral values, as well as a connection to nature. He was known for his dreadlocks, which he saw as a symbol of his commitment to his faith and his belief in the power of natural beauty.

Marley's hobbies reveal a personality characterized by a deep commitment to social justice, unity, and spiritual values. His love of music, soccer, and Rastafarianism were all ways for him to express his beliefs and connect with others who shared his passion for equality, freedom, and love.

Our hobbies can reveal a lot about our personalities, interests, and values, even if they don't have a direct connection to our work or professional lives. In fact, our hobbies can be a way for us to express different parts of ourselves that may not be fully represented in our day-to-day work.

'WHO YOU COULD BE?'

In the Bhagavad Gita, Arjuna is asked a deep question that makes him question who he is and what his life's purpose is. As a warrior on the verge of battle, he is asked to consider who he could be, beyond his current role and identity.

At this key moment, Arjuna sees a vision of his highest potential. This vision goes beyond his limited sense of self and shows him more about who he really is. He is being asked to see himself in a way that fits with his divine purpose and the ultimate truth of the universe.

The story of Arjuna's journey is a powerful reminder that we all have the potential that is just waiting to be found and used. It is a call to wake up to our highest selves, let go of our limiting beliefs and fears, and embrace a vision of ourselves that is in line with our deepest values and goals.

The question of who we could be is not one that can be answered easily or quickly. It requires us to go on a journey of self-discovery, look into our deepest desires and motivations, and face the unknown with courage and determination.

Just as Arjuna had to face his fears and doubts before he could embrace his true potential, we must be willing to face the obstacles and challenges that stand in the way of our personal growth and self-realization. This journey of self-discovery can be difficult and uncomfortable, but it is also incredibly rewarding. By letting go of our limiting beliefs and fears, we open ourselves up to new possibilities and experiences that we may have never thought possible. It is a journey that requires patience, perseverance, and a willingness to learn and grow every step of the way.

Ultimately, who we could be reflects our highest selves, the true essence of our being that is connected to the divine and the universe at large. It is a picture of ourselves that is full of meaning, purpose, and the limitless potential of the human spirit. The journey of self-discovery can be hard, but it leads to a life of purpose, fulfilment, and inner peace in the end.

The idea of "Who you could be" is one that is rooted in the concept of personal growth and self-improvement. It is a question that encourages us to explore our own potential and to imagine the person we could become if we were to tap into our unique talents and abilities.

When we look to JK Rowling as an example, we see someone who epitomizes this idea of self-realization. Even though she had many problems and setbacks along the way, she never forgot how much she loved writing and how much she believed in herself. Through her dedication and hard work, she could bring to life some of the most famous and beloved characters in modern literature, inspiring many readers to follow their own dreams and goals. JK Rowling's success story is a testament to the power of perseverance and self-belief, showing us that with determination and a clear vision of what we want to achieve, we can overcome any obstacle and reach our full potential. Her journey reminds us that the road to success is rarely easy, but it is always worth pursuing if we are passionate about our goals and willing to put in the effort required to achieve them.

In considering the question of "Who you could be," it is important to remember that the answer is different for each person. We all have our own unique strengths and weaknesses, and our paths to self-improvement will be equally varied. But by taking the time to reflect on our own values, goals, and aspirations, we can begin to chart a course towards becoming the person we want to become.

This journey of self-discovery and personal growth requires both introspection and action. It involves taking stock of our current situation and identifying areas where we could improve, as well as setting specific goals and developing a plan to achieve them. Along the way, we may face setbacks and challenges, but it is through these experiences that we learn and grow the most. It's important to remember that self-improvement is a lifelong journey, and it requires patience, perseverance, and self-compassion. By embracing the process and staying committed to our goals, we can continue to evolve and become the best version of ourselves.

Whether we are inspired by the example of JK Rowling or by the countless other individuals who have achieved great things through hard work and determination, we can all take steps to become the best versions of ourselves.

NEVER DOUBT YOUR GUT INSTINCTS

Your gut instincts are often based on subconscious processing of information and experiences that you may not even be aware of, so it's important to trust them. However, it's also important to recognize when your biases or emotions may be clouding your judgement and to take a step back before making any major decisions.

To understand gut instincts, let's take the example of a father. We could have taken the example of a mother, but we will take the example of a father because, in the greatness of a mother, often we ignore the contribution of a father. While the mother-child relationship is often highlighted in discussions about parenting, the role of fathers should not be overlooked.

The role of a father is one that carries with it a great deal of responsibility, both in public and private. Fathers are very important to their children's lives because they set a good example for them and help them with their feelings and decisions.

Some men find the prospect of fatherhood intimidating, particularly if they have never had a strong father figure to look up to. But it is often said that a person's intuition can guide them in powerful ways, even if they have had no training or experience.

With a father who may not have had a clear roadmap for how to navigate his new role, intuition can prove to be a valuable asset. By drawing on his own instincts and personal values, he can begin to chart a course towards becoming the kind of father he wants to be.

This process begins with a deep sense of self-awareness and a willingness to reflect on one's own experiences and beliefs. By taking the time to examine his own attitude towards fatherhood and the kind of relationship he wants to have with his child, a father can begin to develop a clear sense of direction. This kind of self-reflection can also help a dad figure out where he might need more help or resources, like parenting classes or therapy.

By combining his intuition with a willingness to learn and grow, a father can become a confident and effective parent who can give his child the love, guidance, and support they need to thrive.

Whether in public or in private, a father's behavior serves as a model for his child to emulate. By demonstrating kindness, respect, and empathy towards others, a father can instill these same values in his child, setting them on a path towards success in all areas of life.

Even though fathers are very important in shaping the lives of their children, many men may find it hard to explain what fatherhood means to them. This could be because fatherhood is a very personal experience that is shaped by many things, such as a person's own upbringing, values, and cultural background.

As a result, even if a man has a deep intuitive understanding of what it means to be a good father, he may find it difficult to put that understanding into words. Fatherhood is a complicated and multifaceted job that includes both practical skills like changing diapers and calming a crying baby and more abstract skills, like patience, empathy, and wisdom.

In fact, a father's intuition can be a powerful tool in the complicated and always-changing world of being a parent. When a father has to make a hard choice or is in a situation he doesn't know much about, his gut instincts can help him make the right choice for himself and his family.

In the book "To Kill a Mockingbird" by Harper Lee, the character of Atticus Finch, a father and lawyer, relies on his intuition to make the right choices for his family and community. He says, ***"Before I can live with other folks, I've got to live with myself. The one thing that doesn't abide by majority rule is a person's conscience."*** Atticus' instincts and conscience proved to be invaluable in both his personal and professional life. He taught his children to be kind and just, and he fought for what was right despite the risks. Atticus Finch was a model father who relied on his intuition to make decisions that would benefit his family and his community.

CREATE A MINDSET OF GROWTH: NURTURE A BELIEF IN YOUR OWN POTENTIAL

As Eleanor Roosevelt once said, ***"The future belongs to those who believe in the beauty of their dreams."*** This quote exemplifies the idea that success is not just about talent or innate ability, but also about having a mindset that is focused on growth and possibility. In order to achieve our goals, we must first believe that we can reach them.

Adopting a mindset of growth means embracing the idea that we can always learn, improve, and develop new skills. It means reframing challenges as opportunities for growth and seeing setbacks as temporary rather than permanent. It also involves setting ambitious yet achievable goals and being willing to take risks and step outside of our comfort zones.

By nurturing a belief in our own potential, we can overcome self-doubt and fear of failure, and tap into the limitless possibilities that life has to offer. It is a mindset that allows us to pursue our dreams with passion and purpose, and to create a life that is rich with meaning and fulfilment.

In Hindu mythology, there is a story about Lord Ganesha, the elephant-headed god who is widely revered as the remover of obstacles and the patron of arts and sciences. According to the legend, Ganesha was born with a human body and an elephant head because his mother, Goddess Parvati, had created him from clay and brought him to life.

When Ganesha was a young boy, he was tasked with guarding his mother's chambers while she took a bath. However, when Lord Shiva, Parvati's husband, arrived and tried to enter the chambers, Ganesha refused to let him in, not recognizing him as his mother's husband. This led to a heated argument between the two, and in a fit of anger, Lord Shiva beheaded Ganesha.

Distraught over her son's death, Goddess Parvati pleaded with Lord Shiva to bring him back to life. Moved by her devotion, Lord Shiva ordered his followers to bring him the head of the first creature they could find that was sleeping with its head facing north. They returned with the head of an elephant, which Lord Shiva used to bring Ganesha back to life.

The story of Ganesha teaches us several important lessons about creating a mindset of growth and belief in one's own potential. First, it highlights the importance of having an open mind and being willing to learn and adapt. Ganesha initially failed to recognize Lord Shiva because he had never seen him before, but he could overcome his ignorance and become more knowledgeable because of their interaction.

Second, the story emphasizes the importance of resilience and perseverance in the face of setbacks and obstacles. Ganesha was beheaded, but he could come back to life and continue on his path, demonstrating an unwavering belief in his own potential and ability to overcome adversity.

Finally, the story underscores the idea that our unique qualities and attributes are what make us special and enable us to achieve great things. Ganesha's elephant head, which initially set him apart and made him an object of ridicule, ultimately became a source of his strength and power, enabling him to become one of the most beloved and revered gods in Hindu mythology.

As the famous philosopher Aristotle once said, ***"We are what we repeatedly do. Excellence, then, is not an act, but a habit."*** This quote emphasizes the importance of consistency in developing a growth mindset. Nurturing a belief in our own potential also requires us to challenge our limiting beliefs and overcome our fears of failure. It means taking risks, stepping outside of our comfort zones, and being willing to learn from our mistakes. As Albert Einstein said, ***"A person who never made a mistake never tried anything new."*** This highlights the importance of embracing failure as a natural part of the learning process and using it as an opportunity to grow and improve.

Ultimately, creating a mindset of growth and belief in our own potential is a powerful tool for achieving our goals and unlocking our full potential. As the famous motivational speaker, Les Brown once said, ***"You are never too old to set another goal or to dream a new dream."*** This quote reminds us that no matter how old we are or how many times we may have failed, we always have the power to believe in ourselves and pursue our dreams.

DO WHAT IS MORAL AND HELPFUL FOR THE SOCIETY. DON'T BE A BLUNDER TO SOCIETY

The concept of doing what you feel like doing is a complex and multifaceted idea that has been explored by philosophers, psychologists, and social scientists for many years. At its core, this idea suggests that individuals should be free to pursue their own desires and goals and that this pursuit can lead to greater fulfilment, happiness, and success.

However, the idea of doing what you feel like doing also raises important questions about the role of individuals in society and how our actions can affect the well-being of others. While it is true that pursuing one's own desires and goals can lead to personal fulfilment, it is also important to consider the broader social and ethical implications of our actions.

For example, if an individual feels like engaging in behaviours that are harmful or destructive to others, such as stealing, cheating, or engaging in violent behaviour, it is clear that such actions would be detrimental to society. In this sense, the idea of doing what you feel like doing must be balanced with the recognition of our responsibilities to others, and the need to consider the impact of our actions on those around us.

Furthermore, the concept of doing what you feel like doing can also be influenced by social and cultural factors. For example, if an individual grows up in a culture that values material wealth and consumerism, they may be more likely to pursue these goals at the expense of other values such as community, compassion, and environmental sustainability. In this sense, the idea of doing what you feel like doing must also be understood in broader social and cultural influences.

The concept of suffering as the "truest truth" of life is a philosophical perspective that has been explored by many thinkers throughout history. At its core, this idea suggests that suffering is an inherent and unavoidable aspect of the human condition and that it is through our experiences of pain, loss, and hardship that we come to understand the nature of existence itself.

One way to approach this idea is to consider the role that suffering plays in shaping our perceptions of reality. When we experience pain or difficulty, we are forced to confront the limits of our own strength, resilience, and understanding. We are humbled by the enormity of the challenges we face, and we are forced to grapple with questions of meaning, purpose, and mortality.

This confrontation with suffering can be a deeply transformative experience. It can force us to reevaluate our priorities, find new sources of strength and resilience, and deepen our empathy and compassion for others who are also struggling. In this way, suffering can be seen as a catalyst for growth and self-discovery, helping us to become more fully human in the face of life's many challenges.

As the renowned writer and theologian, Henri Nouwen, once said, ***"The great challenge of life is to claim our own place in the world despite all the forces that seek to pull us away from it."*** This highlights the idea that suffering can serve as a force that challenges us to find our place in the world, and to become more human.

When we face challenges and hardships in life, we are often forced to confront our own limitations and vulnerabilities and to accept that we cannot control everything in our lives. This can be a painful and humbling experience, but it can also be a powerful opportunity for growth and self-discovery.

As the philosopher, Friedrich Nietzsche once said, ***"That which does not kill us makes us stronger."*** By facing and overcoming adversity, we can develop a sense of inner strength and resilience that allows us to navigate life's challenges with greater ease and confidence.

The idea that the tragedy of a self-conscious being produces inevitable suffering is a profound insight into the human condition. As self-conscious beings, we are aware of our own mortality and limitations, and this awareness can lead to a sense of existential angst and despair. This suffering can motivate the desire for selfish, immediate gratification, as individuals seek to alleviate their pain through short-term pleasures.

However, as the passage notes, sacrifice and work serve far more effectively than impulsive pleasure at keeping suffering at bay. By accepting the limitations of our existence and working to improve ourselves and our world, we can find meaning and purpose in life, and contribute to the well-being of others.

Yet, the problem of evil must be considered. The world is dead set against us, and man's inhumanity to man can compound the suffering inherent in the human condition. Thus, the problem of sacrifice becomes even more complex, as we must not only address mortal limitations but also the problem of evil.

In this sense, sacrifice involves not only offering and giving up material goods but also working to alleviate the suffering caused by the inhumanity of others. By recognizing the interconnectedness of all beings and working to promote compassion and justice, we can contribute to the alleviation of suffering in the world.

Expedient actions are immediate and impulsive, providing temporary relief without deeper significance. In contrast, meaningful actions involve organizing what would otherwise be expedient into a symphony of Being, as exemplified in Beethoven's "Ode to Joy". This symphony arises from the perfectly functioning harmony of many levels of Being, from atomic microcosm to cosmos. In this harmony, every action at each level beautifully facilitates actions at all other levels, resulting in redemption and reconciliation across the past, present, and future.

In conclusion, the question of "Who we are" is a complex and multifaceted one, and there is no easy answer. However, by tapping into our own intuition and pursuing our passions, we can begin to uncover the answers that lie within us.

Believing in our gut instincts can be a powerful tool for self-discovery, helping us to stay true to our values and make choices that align with our deepest desires. This can be especially important when faced with difficult decisions or uncertain situations, allowing us to stay focused on what truly matters and to chart a course that feels authentic and fulfilling. It's important to remember that self-discovery is a lifelong journey, and our understanding of ourselves will continue to evolve over time. By embracing this process and remaining open to new experiences and perspectives, we can continue to grow and learn more about who we are and what we want out of life.

Likewise, pursuing our passions can be a powerful way to uncover our true selves. When we engage in activities that we are passionate about, we tap into a deep sense of purpose and meaning, allowing us to explore our strengths and weaknesses, our likes and dislikes, and ultimately to better understand who we are and what we want out of life. It's also important to surround ourselves with people who support and encourage our self-discovery journey. Additionally, taking time for self-reflection and introspection can help us gain clarity on our thoughts, feelings, and desires, enabling us to make more informed decisions about our lives.

Of course, finding ourselves is not always an easy journey. It may require us to take risks, face our fears, and push ourselves beyond our comfort zones. However, by embracing the power of our intuition and our passions, we can unlock the inner resources that we need to thrive in all areas of our lives.

Ultimately, the journey of self-discovery is a deeply personal one, and there is no single right way to approach it. However, by staying true to ourselves, pursuing our passions, and listening to our own intuition, we can begin to uncover the answers that we seek and live a life that is truly authentic, fulfilling, and meaningful.

Before we end, I want to share one more story with you on a very basic question, 'Who you could be?'

The idea of "Who you could be" was one that deeply intrigued Roberto. He had always been an avid learner, but this concept seemed to take the idea of education to a completely different level. It was as if there was a secret knowledge that he was expected to uncover—something that would turn him into the best version of himself.

On one particular afternoon, as he walked through his neighbourhood, he encountered an elderly man who had a wise and gentle air about him. Without any prompting, the man asked him, "What do you think you could become if you were to unleash your full potential?"

Roberto was taken aback by the question, but he couldn't help but feel compelled to answer. He searched his mind for an answer, but nothing came to him. He felt as if he had come to a dead end.

The man seemed to sense his confusion and said, "Don't worry, you don't need to find the answer today. All I want you to do is to keep asking yourself this question as you go through life. The answer will come in its own time." With that, the man gave Roberto a knowing look and walked away.

Roberto stood there for a few moments, contemplating the older man's words. He could feel a sense of peace settle over him as he took in the idea of personal growth and self-improvement. He realized that he didn't need to rush the process—all he had to do was to keep asking himself this question, and gradually, he would uncover the answer. As Roberto continued his walk, he felt a new sense of purpose take hold of him. He knew that he had been given a gift, a catalyst for change that would ignite a fire within him. He had always been an introspective person, but this encounter had opened up a new avenue of self-discovery for him.

Over the next few days and weeks, Roberto would often find himself lost in thought, considering what he could become if he unleashed his full potential. He realized that he had been holding himself back, settling for mediocrity instead of striving for greatness.

One day, Roberto decided to take action. He sat down with a pen and paper and began to write out his goals and dreams, no matter how big or small they may seem. He was determined to start living the life he had always wanted, and he knew that it all began with taking the first step.

As the days went by, Roberto began to notice a change within himself. He felt more confident, more in control of his life. He was making progress towards his goals, one step at a time. He knew that he still had a long way to go, but he was excited for the journey ahead.

Years later, as Roberto looked back on his life, he realized that it had all started with that chance encounter with the wise old man. He had never forgotten the lesson he had learned that day, and he had kept asking himself the question that had sparked his transformation. He had become the best version of himself, and he knew that it was all thanks to that one moment of inspiration.

2

YOU ARE A PIECE OF ART: HANDLE YOURSELF WITH CARE!

I recall when there was a time when I was indulging in a podcast that delved into the intricacies of life philosophy. The radio jockey was particularly adept at stirring up thought-provoking questions that would challenge even the most steadfast of beliefs. On that day, he posed a question that seemed simple at first glance but had a profound impact on my perspective.

The question was straightforward: "What would you do if you were awarded 5 crore rupees the next morning, when you open your eyes?" Naturally, most people would answer that they would spend the money on various things they had always wanted to buy.

But then the RJ rephrased the question and added a twist: "What would you choose if you were awarded 5 crores rupees in cash or a chance to open your eyes the next morning?" Suddenly, the answer wasn't as clear-cut.

The RJ's question opened my eyes to the fact that, while money is important, there are things in life that are much more valuable. We should be grateful for everyday we get to wake up and experience life, and treasure the simple moments that make life worth living.

In our modern society, self-discovery and self-worth have become highly valued aspects of personal development. However, as we strive to understand ourselves better, we may ask ourselves how far this process should go.

It is common to advise young people to pursue their passions and work hard to achieve their goals. The implication here is that the most important answers lie deep within oneself and that taking the time to explore one's priorities, passions, and values is crucial for success in life.

"I am the master of my fate
I am the captain of my soul."

– William Ernest Henley

As we enter adulthood, we are encouraged to sit down and ask ourselves some of life's most profound questions: What is the purpose of our existence? What do we want out of life? What are the things we truly value, independent of the opinions of others?

These questions are not only important for personal development but also for determining our place in the world. But these are the things that are applicable when the setting is acceptable. Everything that is happening around you is going according to your goals, and your moral rights have not been compromised. What would you do with your time and energy if you lost everything you owned? If this were to happen, what would you consider to be your true passion?

These are questions that most of us never have to face until we come across a situation that completely changes the course of our lives. Such a life-altering event can happen—an accident, the sudden death of a loved one, natural disaster, or simply a book that you read called "Man's Search for Meaning".

This book is about Viktor Frankl's journey through the Holocaust and his search for meaning in life amidst unimaginable suffering. He goes further to describe how he could find hope even in the darkest moments. It is one of those stories which can leave you speechless yet inspire you at the same time. As you read it, you may feel compelled to reflect on your own life and question what true freedom and happiness mean to you.

It is easy to feel overwhelmed when faced with such an event, but Viktor Frankl's experience has taught us the power of repentance and resilience. Viktor's experiences during the Holocaust were nothing short of traumatic. He was stripped of his possessions, his freedom, and even his identity. Along with his fellow prisoners, he was subjected to inhumane conditions, physical abuse, and constant fear of death. Despite all of this, Viktor refused to give up hope. He found immense strength in his ideals and his belief that there was a purpose to his suffering.

One example of Viktor's inspiring resilience was when he was tasked with the job of cleaning out the latrines. Many prisoners found this task to be repulsive and degrading, and as a result, they would often give up and succumb to their circumstances. However, Viktor saw this task as an opportunity to serve his fellow prisoners. He would often use this time to speak to his fellow prisoners, offer words of encouragement, and even share his food. Through his actions, Viktor could inspire those around him to find meaning in their suffering.

Another example of Viktor's inspiring spirit was when he learned that his wife had died in a concentration camp. Despite being shattered by this news, Viktor refused to let go of his ideals. He knew that his wife would want him to continue living his life with purpose and meaning. From that day on, Viktor made a vow to himself that he would use his experiences to help others find hope and meaning in their own lives.

The thing about this is that the circumstances can change, but how you react to it is the overall learning behind your own life.

'How you react to the situation is what defines you the best.'

For Viktor, the key to surviving the Holocaust was not just physical strength, but mental resilience. He found strength in his ideals, his belief in the power of the human spirit, and his determination to find meaning in his suffering. His experiences showed us that no matter what happens to us in life, we can always choose our response to it.

As Viktor and his fellow prisoners were liberated from the concentration camp, he made a vow to himself that he would use his experiences to help others find meaning and hope in their lives. He went on to become a renowned psychiatrist and wrote the book "Man's Search for Meaning" as a testament to his experiences.

Through his words and actions, Viktor provided us with a powerful reminder of the resilience of the human spirit. He showed us that even in the most challenging situations, we have the power to find hope, meaning, and purpose in our lives. His legacy continues to inspire and guide us today, reminding us that we can overcome any obstacle and find joy and fulfillment in our lives.

> ***"Not everything is crystal clear, sometime you need to work with coal to discover the diamond."***

One quote that comes to mind in this context is attributed to Thomas Edison:

> ***"Opportunity is missed by most people because it is dressed in overalls and looks like work."***

This quote emphasizes the importance of hard work and perseverance in achieving success. Edison, who is widely regarded as one of the greatest inventors in history, understood that the road to success was neither difficult nor straightforward. Instead, he believed that success was the result of a willingness to work hard, to learn from failures, and to persist in the face of obstacles.

From a philosophical perspective, this quote reflects the idea that success is not simply a matter of luck or talent, but the result of a sustained effort to improve oneself and one's circumstances.

It also highlights the importance of embracing the challenges and difficulties that inevitably arise along the way, rather than shying away from them.

In this sense, the idea that "not everything is crystal clear, sometime you need to work with coal to discover the diamond" is similar to Edison's quote. Both suggest that true success requires a willingness to put in the effort and persevere through challenges, even when things are not immediately clear or easy.

One story from the Bible that supports the idea that success requires hard work and perseverance is the story of Joseph in the Book of Genesis. Joseph was one of the twelve sons of Jacob and was favored by his father. His brothers became jealous of him and sold him into slavery in Egypt. Despite this setback, Joseph worked hard and gained the trust of his master, Potiphar. However, when Potiphar's wife falsely accused him of trying to seduce her, Joseph was thrown into prison.

Even in prison, Joseph did not give up. He continued to work hard and used his skills to interpret dreams for his fellow prisoners. Eventually, word of Joseph's abilities reached Pharaoh, the ruler of Egypt, who summoned Joseph to interpret a troubling dream. Joseph correctly interpreted the dream as a warning of impending famine and advised Pharaoh to store grain in preparation.

Impressed by Joseph's wisdom and abilities, Pharaoh made him second-in-command of all of Egypt. Joseph's hard work and perseverance led him from slavery and imprisonment to a position of great power and influence.

This story illustrates the importance of hard work, even in the face of adversity. Joseph did not let his setbacks defeat him, but continued to work hard and use his skills to better himself and those around him. In the end, his persistence paid off, and he achieved great success.

ASKING FOR HELP IS SOMETIMES ALL YOU NEED TO DO!

We all face situations where we feel stuck, lost, or unsure of what to do next. In such times, it's essential to remind ourselves that seeking help is not a sign of weakness, but a sign of strength and self-awareness. Asking for help is difficult, but it's crucial to understand that we don't have to go through our struggles alone.

It's important to acknowledge that we don't have all the answers, nor do we possess the experience to handle every situation that comes our way.

It's important to surround ourselves with people who can support us when we need it. They may be family members, friends, colleagues, or professionals, like therapists or counselors. Seeking help from these individuals can provide us with a fresh perspective, new ideas, or the emotional support we need to overcome our struggles.

The story of Buddha is a prime example of how seeking help can lead to profound change and growth. Before he became the enlightened teacher we know today, Buddha was a prince who ruled over a kingdom. Despite his privileged position, he felt troubled by the suffering he saw around him. He wanted to understand the nature of suffering and how he could help those who were struggling.

Buddha scoured local libraries, spoke to renowned teachers, and roamed the countryside in search of answers. But each time he was left feeling even more hollow, until finally, he decided to strike out on his own.

He withdrew from society and secluded himself in a simple hut at the edge of the forest. There, he meditated for hours at a time, delving deep into his subconscious, and seeking understanding through self-inquiry. After months of intense contemplation, Buddha had an epiphany that brought clarity to his purpose; he gained insight into the causes of suffering and the path to enlightenment.

Finally, he decided to take matters into his own hands and embarked on a period of intense self-reflection and meditation. Through his own efforts, he gained deep insight into the nature of suffering and the path to liberation.

Buddha's willingness to seek help and his humility in acknowledging that he didn't have all the answers were key factors in his eventual enlightenment. His story shows us that even those who are in positions of power and privilege can benefit from seeking help and being open to learning from others.

Another great example of seeking help when feeling stuck in life is the story of Maya Angelou. Maya Angelou was a renowned American poet, author, and civil rights activist who faced many challenges throughout her life. Despite her accomplishments, she still felt lost and unsure of herself.

In her autobiography, "I Know Why the Caged Bird Sings", Angelou writes about how she sought help when she felt stuck. She writes,

> ***"I know that when I pray, something wonderful happens. Not just to the person or persons for whom I'm praying, but also to something wonderful that happens to me. I'm grateful that I'm heard."***

As Maya Angelou continued to face life's challenges, she found solace in the belief that there was a higher power watching over her, and that her prayers would be answered in some form or another. This belief gave her the strength to persevere through difficult times and to continue pursuing her dreams.

Angelou's story is a testament to the power of faith and the importance of seeking help when feeling lost or stuck in life. It reminds us that we are not alone in our struggles and that there is always someone or something we can turn to for support. Whether it's through prayer, talking to a friend or family member, or seeking professional help, reaching out for assistance can make all the difference in overcoming life's challenges.

Moreover, Angelou's story also teaches us that sometimes the best way to help ourselves is to help others. By praying for others, Angelou not only found comfort for herself, but she also helped to uplift and support those around her. This act of selflessness and compassion not only benefited those she prayed for, but it also helped to strengthen her own faith and sense of purpose.

Maya Angelou's story serves as a powerful reminder that seeking help and having faith in something greater than ourselves can help us to overcome life's challenges and find meaning and purpose in our lives. It is a lesson that we can all learn from and apply to our own lives, no matter what struggles we may be facing. As Maya Angelou's story shows us, seeking help is not a sign of weakness, but a sign of strength and courage. It takes strength to admit that we don't have all the answers and to ask for assistance. By doing so, we can gain new perspectives, overcome our challenges, and ultimately find greater peace and happiness in life.

On the other hand, there are those who believe in the power of self-reliance and taking matters into their own hands. Ralph Waldo Emerson, an American essayist and philosopher, is a prime example of this mindset. In his essay "Self-Reliance," he writes, ***"Trust thyself: every heart vibrates to that iron string."***

Emerson argued that, too often, people look to others for guidance and validation, rather than trusting their own inner voice.

Another example of this mindset can be found in the story of Christopher McCandless, a young man who famously ventured into the Alaskan wilderness alone, seeking to live off the land and escape from society. In his journal, McCandless wrote, ***"Happiness is only real when shared."*** However, he ultimately paid the price for his stubborn self-reliance and lack of preparation, dying of starvation in the wilderness.

These examples illustrate the conflicting beliefs about seeking help and relying solely on oneself. While some, like Maya Angelou, believe in the power of seeking help, others, like Ralph Waldo Emerson and Christopher McCandless, believe in the power of self-reliance. Ultimately, the choice of whether to seek help or rely on oneself is a personal one, and there is no one-size-fits-all answer. As with many things in life, balance and moderation are key.

But then comes another scenario that differs totally from the others. The procrastinators.

Here, even when one has all the help one needs, progress can still be hindered by a lack of willingness to take action. This is exemplified in the story of Anne Lamott, an American novelist, and a non-fiction writer. In her book "Bird by Bird," Lamott discusses writing and the struggles that can come with it. She writes, ***"The only way I can get anything written at all is to write really, really shitty first drafts."***

Lamott acknowledges that the creative process can be challenging, but emphasizes the importance of taking action and getting started, even if the first attempt is not perfect. However, even with this knowledge, she admits to struggling with procrastination and self-doubt.

As writers, we often fall into the trap of waiting for the perfect moment, the perfect idea, or the perfect opening line. We convince ourselves that we cannot start writing until everything is just right. But there is no such thing as perfection in writing. Every great masterpiece began as a messy, imperfect first draft.

Lamott encourages writers to embrace the messiness of the creative process and to allow themselves to write poorly at first. She likens the process to that of a birdhouse builder, who works slowly and steadily, piece by piece until the structure is complete. The same can be said for writing—it's not about writing a perfect first draft, but about putting in the work, piece by piece, until the final product is complete. Of course, this is easier said than done.

> ***"Procrastination and self-doubt are the most powerful obstacles to overcome."***

One of the main reasons that procrastination and self-doubt are so powerful is that they often feed off of each other. For example, an individual who is experiencing self-doubt may be more likely to procrastinate because they don't feel confident in their ability to complete the task at hand. Similarly, procrastination can lead to feelings of self-doubt because the individual may feel like they are not making progress or living up to their potential.

Overcoming procrastination and self-doubt requires a combination of self-awareness, goal-setting, and self- discipline. The first step is to identify the root causes of these obstacles and address them directly. For example, if an individual is procrastinating because they feel overwhelmed by a large task, they can break it down into smaller, more manageable steps. If self-doubt is the issue, they can work on building their confidence through positive self-talk, affirmations, or seeking support from a mentor or coach.

Lamott suggests setting small, manageable goals for oneself, such as writing for just 15 minutes a day. She also recommends finding a supportive writing community, whether that be through a writing group or online forum, to help combat feelings of isolation and self-doubt.

The most important thing is simply to start. To sit down at one's desk, put pen to paper or fingers to keyboard, and begin. It may not be perfect, and it may not even be good, but it's a starting point. And from there, the real work can begin.

Many people may have access to resources and support but may still struggle to take action because of fear, anxiety, or self-doubt. In these cases, it's important to recognize that seeking help is only one part of the equation. As the author, Mark Twain, once said,

> ***"The secret of getting ahead is getting started. The secret of getting started is breaking your complex, overwhelming tasks into small manageable tasks, and then starting on the first one."***

While having help and support is valuable, ultimately it is up to the individual to take responsibility and make progress toward their desired outcome.

DON'T BE BLIND WHILE FOLLOWING THE ADVICE!

American educator Benjamin Franklin, states, ***"Tell me and I forget. Teach me and I remember. Involve me and I learn."*** This quote highlights the importance of actively engaging in the learning process and not simply relying on others to tell you what to do.

Let's begin with a story.

A little boy was alone in his room, studying fervently for his first big test. He had been given a stack of textbooks and notes and had been warned to take the day off from school in order to devote himself entirely to his studies. He had done as he was told, and now was intently going through every page of his textbooks, memorizing the facts and equations, and making sure he was ready for the moment of truth.

But little did he know of the fateful path he was about to take. It all started when he stepped into the examination hall on the day of the exam, eagerly looking around for familiar faces. That was when he spotted the other boy, already sitting in his seat and looking confident, yet strangely out of place. He looked like a complete stranger, yet he had a familiarity about him that made the little boy feel oddly at ease.

He decided to take a chance and started a conversation with the stranger, and he was a student from the same school, albeit a few grades ahead. The other boy told him he had been studying for the same test, and they started discussing the material he had been studying.

The little boy was captivated by the other student's knowledge and experience, and he began to trust his judgement without question. He believed him when he said that some answers contained in the textbook were wrong and that studying too much wouldn't help him. He also followed his suggestion to focus on the more abstract questions, convinced that his approach was the right one.

On the day of the exam, the little boy blindly followed the advice of the strange boy, trusting that he knew better. He was so sure of himself that he could answer most of the questions without even reading the material properly. But his confidence was misplaced, as soon after the exam was over he realized that he had failed miserably.

He had done exactly as the stranger had told him, without considering the potential consequences. He had followed his advice blindly, without thinking of the potential harm it could bring. He had been too trusting and too naïve, and he now faced the bitter consequences of his decision.

The little boy was devastated. He had failed the test and all his dreams had been shattered. He had let himself be misled and had gained nothing from it. He was filled with regret and shame, but he also learned an important lesson. He would never again be so reckless and naïve. He would never again trust someone blindly as he had done with the strange boy. From now on, he would rely solely on himself and think twice before making any decisions.

The American writer and philosopher, Ralph Waldo Emerson, once said,

> ***"The only person you are destined to become is the person you decide to be."***

BE RESPONSIBLE FOR WHO YOU ARE AND WHAT YOU WANT IN YOUR LIFE!

Taking responsibility for your own decisions and actions is essential for success. It requires perseverance, determination, and a willingness to take risks. By taking ownership of your choices and their consequences, you are setting yourself up for success in life.

One example of someone who took responsibility for their own actions is Oprah Winfrey. As a young girl, Oprah faced many challenges growing up in poverty with little parental guidance or support. Despite this difficult upbringing, she used her passion and ambition to create her own destiny. She chose to pursue an education and eventually became one of the most influential women in media history. Through her hard work and dedication to self-improvement, Oprah achieved success by taking personal responsibility for her decisions and actions.

Another example of a successful person who took responsibility for their own actions is Steve Jobs. Jobs was passionate about computing technology from an early age but faced many obstacles along his journey to success such as being fired from Apple (the company he co-founded). In spite of these setbacks, Jobs was persistent in his pursuit of creating innovative products that changed the world forever through his company Apple Inc. Jobs demonstrated that no matter how many times you fail or get knocked down, it's important to keep pushing forward and taking responsibility for the outcomes that result from your decisions and actions.

The list goes on. Jeff Bezos is another clear example of someone who took responsibility for their own actions and decisions and made something incredible out of it—Amazon is now one of the largest e-commerce companies in the world. JK Rowling had an incredibly tough time financially before writing 'Harry Potter' but she never gave up on her dream despite numerous rejections from publishers; she eventually went on to become one of the best-selling authors.

These examples illustrate the power that comes with taking responsibility for one's own decisions and actions. Taking personal accountability allows us to learn from our mistakes while also inspiring us to strive toward greatness no matter what challenges we face along the way!

CONFUSED? LIFE IS INDEED CONFUSING

Knowing whom to follow and whom not to follow can be a challenging task, and it requires a combination of critical thinking, experience, and intuition. If you really want to get to the bottom of this, here are some tips on how to make wise decisions when choosing whom to follow:

1. Consider the person's track record: Look at the person's past behavior and how they have dealt with similar situations. Do they have a history of making sound decisions, or have they made poor decisions that led to negative consequences? Assessing a person's track record can give you a clue whether they are trustworthy and reliable.
2. Assess the person's expertise: Evaluate the person's knowledge and experience in the area that you're seeking advice on. Are they well-informed and knowledgeable, or are they speaking from a place of limited experience

or understanding? The person's level of expertise can indicate whether their advice is reliable and relevant.

3. Consider the person's motivation: Try to understand the person's motivation for giving you advice. Are they genuinely interested in helping you, or do they have a hidden agenda? The person's motivation can affect the quality and usefulness of their advice.
4. Seek diverse perspectives: It's always a good idea to seek advice from multiple sources to get a range of perspectives. Consider seeking advice from people with different backgrounds, experiences, and points of view. This approach can help you make a more informed decision by considering multiple perspectives.
5. Trust your intuition: Finally, trust your gut feeling when it comes to deciding whom to follow. If something doesn't feel right about the person's advice, or if you have a sense that something is off, it's best to listen to your intuition and seek advice from someone else.

Life can indeed be confusing, and this quote by American author and poet, Maya Angelou, captures this sentiment well: "***I've learned that no matter what happens, or how bad it seems today, life does go on, and it will be better tomorrow.***"

So, when you're feeling confused or overwhelmed, remember that life is a continuous process of growth and change, and there is always the potential for things to get better.

> ***"You yourself, as much as anybody in the entire universe, deserve your love and affection."***
>
> –Buddha

3

BEYOND FRIENDSHIP: THE POWER OF AUTHENTIC CONNECTIONS IN PERSONAL GROWTH

Let's begin our new topic with the famous book "The Alchemist" by Paulo Coelho.

In the book, the main character Santiago embarks on a journey to fulfil his personal legend or life's purpose. Along the way, he meets a variety of people who help him on his journey, including a crystal merchant. The merchant teaches Santiago the importance of making genuine connections with others, stating, ***"I don't know if the shepherd's wife would like it if I wept because she refuses to marry me, but I do know that the crystal merchant wouldn't like it if, one day, I just decided to leave without knowing why I was doing it."***

The crystal merchant, who has been in business for years, understands the importance of cultivating relationships with his customers in order to maintain their loyalty and trust. Similarly, Santiago comes to realize that the relationships he forms along his journey are just as important as the destination itself.

The relationships Santiago forms with others teach him to find comfort in uncertainty, remain open-minded and take risks. He learns to trust his intuition and courageously pursue his dreams despite the unknowns. For example, when he meets an Englishman who claims to turn lead into gold, Santiago is initially skeptical but decides to take a risk and travel with him, regardless. Perhaps this is why the alchemist says ***"When you want something, all the universe conspires in helping you achieve it."***

Santiago also comes across a gypsy woman who reads his palm and tells him that he must search for his treasure at the pyramids of Egypt. Initially scared of taking such a journey alone, Santiago ultimately draws on the strength of the relationships he has formed throughout his journey thus far and musters up enough courage to make the leap. Along each step of his journey, Santiago's relationships provide guidance and support that give him the confidence he needs to continue onward toward achieving personal growth.

At the end of "The Alchemist," Santiago is reunited with Fatima—the shepherd's daughter whom he had grown close with during his travels—and declares her as "his one true love". By doing so, Santiago recognizes that developing meaningful connections with others can be just as fulfilling as achieving our goals. Through this relationship and through those before this one, Santiago learned how powerful companionship can be in helping us reach our full potential—and no matter what kind of journey we are on or what kind of goal we are striving for—cultivating authentic relationships will always serve us well in our process of personal growth.

The book also emphasizes the importance of authenticity in these connections. The alchemist tells him, ***"Everyone seems to have a clear idea of how other people should lead their lives, but none about his or her own."***

It is often said that friendship is one of the most powerful forces in the world, and this is certainly the case when it comes to personal growth. Friendship is often seen as a cornerstone of life, providing an important source of support, comfort, and understanding. But what if there is something even more powerful than friendship? Something that can take us beyond friendship and into a realm of deeper, more authentic connections?

The power of authentic connections in personal growth is something that has been explored and discussed by philosophers, psychologists, and mystics throughout recorded history. As the ancient Greek philosopher Aristotle once said, ***"The energy of the soul is the realization of our potential."***

Authentic connections are not only beneficial to our personal growth, but they can also help us build meaningful relationships with others. By engaging in authentic conversations and interactions, we create the opportunity for genuine understanding and connection. It is through these kinds of interactions that we can develop strong and lasting bonds of friendship—bonds that allow us to truly appreciate the value of each other's existence.

One way to access this type of connection is through meditation or contemplation. By taking time out from our busy lives to sit quietly and reflect on ourselves, our thoughts, feelings, experiences, and beliefs, we gain insight into who we truly are as individuals. This introspection allows us to discover our authentic selves and gain a deeper understanding of our true potential. This helps us strengthen our relationships with others by allowing us to appreciate the unique gifts they bring into our lives.

The power of authentic connections in personal growth has been explored by great spiritual teachers such as Lao Tzu who believed that ***"The journey of a thousand miles begins with one step"***. Similarly, the Dalai Lama has spoken about how "true happiness comes from having an inner peace which results from cultivating a deep appreciation for life"—emphasizing the importance of self-awareness in achieving genuine contentment in life.

In order to get an understanding of how authentic connections can lead to personal growth, it is necessary to look at the concept of relationships. A relationship is an important aspect of life, and it can often be a powerful driver of personal growth. A relationship between two people is an expression of connection, and the quality of that connection can provide the foundation for significant growth.

An important aspect of a relationship is the idea of trust, and this is particularly true when it comes to authentic connections. Trust is essential for any relationship to work and is particularly important for authentic connections. When two people trust each other, they can open up to each other and express themselves more authentically. This can lead to a deeper understanding of each other and a greater sense of connection.

Authentic connections can also lead to increased self-awareness, as they provide an opportunity to reflect on our own behavior and motivations. By engaging in authentic connections, we can gain a better understanding of ourselves and our own thoughts, feelings, and actions. This is the key to true personal growth, as it allows us to take ownership of our own lives and make positive changes.

By engaging in authentic connections, we can also begin to explore our own spiritual journey and discover our own unique spiritual path.

Mystics, saints, and sages throughout history have used stories and myths to explore the power of authentic connections in personal growth. Many of these stories and myths involve a journey of self-discovery, in which the protagonist embarks on a quest to discover themselves and their true sense of purpose in life. A prime example of this is the ancient Greek myth of Psyche, in which a young woman embarks on a quest to become reunited with her beloved. Along the way, she is confronted with a number of tests and challenges, which she must overcome in order to reach her ultimate goal. Ultimately, Psyche succeeds in her quest, and her experiences serve to teach her invaluable lessons about herself, her relationships, and her unique purpose in life.

This story illustrates how authentic connections can lead to personal growth. The power of authentic connections in personal growth is something that has been explored and discussed throughout history. As the famous philosopher and poet John Donne once wrote, ***"No man is an island, entire of itself; every man is a piece of the continent, a part of the main."***

BE VULNERABLE AND LET THE MAGIC WORK

The idea that vulnerability is a key component of building authentic connections is echoed in many famous books and mythologies, including "The Odyssey" by Homer.

In the story, the main character Odysseus embarks on a long and difficult journey home after fighting in the Trojan War. Along the way, he encounters a variety of challenges and obstacles, including the cyclops Polyphemus. In order to escape from the Cyclops' cave, Odysseus comes up with a plan to blind him. However, in order to execute the plan, Odysseus must reveal his true identity to Polyphemus.

This moment of vulnerability ultimately allows Odysseus to connect with Polyphemus on a deeper level, as he appeals to his sense of hospitality and eventually gains his trust. The moment of vulnerability and honesty ultimately helps Odysseus to escape from the Cyclops and continue on his journey.

Just like Odysseus, many other heroes such as Achilles and Aeneas also employ their courage and vulnerability to gain an understanding for themselves and others along their respective journeys. Furthermore, characters like Beowulf use their fearlessness when facing Grendel's mother and Medusa respectively to demonstrate their bravery and openness towards unknowns.

Similarly, in the book "Daring Greatly" by Brené Brown, the author argues that vulnerability is essential to building strong and meaningful connections with others. Brown writes, ***"Vulnerability is the birthplace of love, belonging, joy, courage, empathy, and creativity. It is the source of hope, empathy, accountability, and***

authenticity. If we want greater clarity in our purpose or deeper and more meaningful spiritual lives, vulnerability is the path."

Brown goes on to offer strategies for developing the courage to be vulnerable, such as practicing self-compassion and recognizing that vulnerability is not a weakness, but a strength that allows us to connect more deeply with others. By embracing vulnerability and sharing our innermost thoughts and feelings with others, we can build authentic connections that help us to grow and thrive.

To expand on the idea of vulnerability in building authentic connections, let's look at the example of Harry Potter from JK Rowling's book series.

Throughout the books, Harry forms deep connections with several characters, including his best friends Ron and Hermione, his mentor Dumbledore, and his godfather Sirius Black. These connections are built on a foundation of trust and vulnerability, as each character shares their innermost thoughts, fears, and hopes with one another.

For example, when Harry is struggling with the weight of his destiny as "the chosen one", he confides in Dumbledore, admitting his fears and doubts. Dumbledore responds with compassion and empathy, offering guidance and support. This moment of vulnerability and honesty strengthens their relationship and ultimately helps Harry to become more confident and resilient.

Similarly, when Harry loses his godfather Sirius, he turns to his friends Ron and Hermione for comfort and support. They listen to him, offer words of encouragement, and hold space for his grief. This moment of vulnerability and connection strengthens their friendship and helps Harry to heal.

Overall, the examples of Harry Potter, Odysseus, and Brené Brown's work all point to the idea that vulnerability is essential to building authentic connections with others. When we are willing to share our true selves with others, we open the door to deeper connections, empathy, and understanding. This can be difficult and scary but ultimately leads to greater growth, fulfillment, and happiness.

There is a growing body of scientific research that supports the idea that vulnerability is essential to building authentic connections with others.

For example, a study published in the journal "Personality and Social Psychology Review" found that vulnerability is a key component of intimacy in romantic relationships. The researchers found that couples who were willing to be vulnerable with one another had stronger relationships and reported higher levels of relationship satisfaction.

Similarly, a study published in the journal "Psychology of Men & Masculinity" found that men who were willing to be vulnerable with their friends reported higher levels of emotional intimacy and social support. The study also found that men who were more willing to express vulnerability had lower levels of anxiety and depression.

These findings are consistent with the idea that vulnerability is essential to building authentic connections and experiencing greater emotional well-being. By being willing to share our innermost thoughts and feelings with others, we create opportunities for empathy, understanding, and mutual support.

In addition, another study published in the journal "Health Psychology" found that people who reported having strong social support networks had lower levels of stress and better physical health outcomes.

FROM HUMAN TO HANUMAN: OVERCOMING OBSTACLES TO FORM AUTHENTIC CONNECTIONS

The story of Hanuman realizing his powers is a well-known tale from Hindu mythology. According to the legend, Hanuman was born to Anjana, a celestial nymph, and Kesari, a monkey king. He was blessed with incredible strength, agility, and intelligence, and was said to have the ability to fly.

However, as a young monkey, Hanuman was not aware of his true potential. He spent his days playing with his monkey friends and causing mischief in the forest.

One day, while playing with his friends, Hanuman saw the sun rising in the sky. Mistaking it for a ripe fruit, he leaped into the air to catch it. However, as he flew higher and higher, he realized that the sun was not a fruit at all, but a fiery ball of gas.

Fearing for his life, Hanuman began to recite the name of Lord Rama, the incarnation of the god Vishnu. As he chanted the name, he felt a surge of power coursing through his body. He realized that he had been blessed with divine strength and abilities and that he was destined for a great purpose.

From that moment on, Hanuman devoted himself to serving Lord Rama and helping him in his quest to rescue his wife Sita from the demon king Ravana. He used his incredible strength and intelligence to overcome obstacles and defeat Ravana's army and ultimately helped Lord Rama reunite with Sita.

The story of Hanuman realizing his powers is a reminder of the importance of recognizing our own unique strengths and abilities. Like Hanuman, we may not always be aware of our true potential, but by remaining open to new experiences and challenges, we can discover our own inner power and use it to achieve great things in life.

But realizing your powers is not enough. You need to be a team member if you really want to achieve your goal.

One aspect of Hanuman's story that could relate to overcoming barriers to authentic connections is his ability to connect with others despite his physical appearance and background. As a monkey, Hanuman was considered an outsider among the gods and goddesses, and his physical appearance often made him the subject of ridicule and rejection.

However, Hanuman's unwavering devotion to Lord Rama and his willingness to serve others eventually won him the respect and admiration of those around him. He formed meaningful connections with other deities and even with ordinary humans who recognized his courage and loyalty.

This story illustrates the importance of persistence and commitment in overcoming barriers to authentic connections. Like Hanuman, we may face rejection or ridicule when trying to form connections with others, but if we remain committed to our values and beliefs, we can ultimately win the trust and respect of those around us.

Additionally, the story of Hanuman also emphasizes the importance of looking beyond external appearances and backgrounds when forming connections with others. Often, our preconceptions and biases can prevent us from seeing the true value and potential of those around us. By recognizing the unique strengths and qualities of each individual, we can form more authentic and meaningful connections with others.

Overall, the story of Hanuman offers a powerful example of overcoming barriers to authentic connections through persistence, commitment, and looking beyond external appearances. By embodying these qualities in our own lives, we can form deeper, more meaningful connections with others and experience greater personal growth and well-being.

> ***'If you want to remain sane in this mad world, keep your connections alive and nurture your relationship with love and care.'***

The concept of nurturing and maintaining authentic connections is an ancient one, and despite the various technological advancements made over centuries, it remains as relevant today as it has ever been. As William Arthur Ward famously said, ***"The mediocre teacher tells. The good teacher explains. The superior teacher demonstrates. The great teacher inspires."*** This quote speaks to the importance of connecting with others and inspiring them to reach their fullest potential.

Throughout the ages, this concept has been explored in myths, stories, and books. In Greek mythology, for example, the tale of Andromeda and Perseus serves as an illustration of the power of authentic connection. Perseus and Andromeda both were fated to be sacrificed, but he saves her from death by slaying the monster Cetus. Throughout their harrowing journey, the two rely on each other for strength and courage. Ultimately, it is their connection that allows them to persevere and ultimately triumph.

A similar theme can be found in the pages of the Bible. In the book of John, Jesus famously says, ***"A new commandment I give to you, that you love one another: just as I have loved you, you also are to love one another."*** Jesus' words are a reminder to us all that the best way to nurture and maintain authentic connections is to show love and kindness to each other.

The concept of nurturing and maintaining authentic connections can also be found in the works of many famous authors. In Jane Austen's classic novel, "Pride and Prejudice", the central theme revolves around the importance of understanding and accepting others despite our differences. Elizabeth Bennet and Mr Darcy, the protagonists of the novel, must overcome their initial dislike of each other in order to find true love and connection. This demonstrates the power of authentic connection and how it can foster growth and understanding.

The metaphor of a garden is often used to represent the concept of nurturing and maintaining authentic connections. Much like a garden, our relationships require ongoing care and nourishment in order to achieve their fullest potential. If we put in the effort to nurture our relationships, we will find that our connections become stronger and more meaningful.

The metaphor of a bridge is also commonly used to represent the concept of authentic connection. Building a bridge of understanding between two people is akin to building a bridge between two destinations. We must be willing to meet each other halfway and work together to bridge the gap between us. This is key to nurturing and maintaining meaningful connections.

Nurturing and maintaining authentic connections is a reminder to us all that we must be willing to put in the effort to cultivate meaningful and lasting connections with others. It is a concept that we should all strive to understand and practice in our own lives. As the old saying goes, ***"It is not a lack of love, but a lack of friendship that makes unhappy marriages."*** Through understanding and compassion, we can nourish our connections and find true and lasting happiness.

When I am talking about this very topic, one book that delves into the importance of nurturing and maintaining authentic connections is "The Little Prince" by Antoine de Saint-Exupéry. The story follows a young prince who travels from planet to planet and encounters various characters, including a fox who teaches him the value of developing a deep and meaningful connection with others.

The fox says to the prince, ***"It is only with the heart that one can see rightly; what is essential is invisible to the eye."*** This quote emphasizes the importance of looking beyond surface-level appearances and connecting with others on a deeper, more meaningful level.

> ***'Make connections that can grow, and do not drag if things are not working.'***

When it comes to building and maintaining connections, it's important to recognize that not every connection is going to be a good fit or last forever. It's essential to focus on quality over quantity and to invest time and effort into the connections that add value to your life, both personally and professionally. Additionally, don't be afraid to let go of connections that no longer serve you or bring negativity into your life. If you find that a particular connection is consistently causing you stress, anxiety, or unhappiness, it may be time to re-evaluate whether it is worthwhile to continue maintaining that connection. Although it is natural for any relationship to experience highs and lows, it is important to recognize when a connection is causing you consistent negative emotions. It is important to prioritize your own mental health and well-being, and sometimes that means letting go of toxic relationships. It can be difficult, but ultimately, it is necessary for your own growth and happiness.

"Eat, Pray, Love" by Elizabeth Gilbert is a good example of a book that investigates the negative impact that toxic relationships have on the personal development of its readers. The author spends the better part of a year travelling through Italy, India, and Indonesia as she writes about her search for inner peace and happiness in her book. Gilbert recounts her struggles with a toxic relationship throughout the entirety of the book, which she eventually comes to realize is holding her back:

"I had actively participated in every moment of the creation of this [toxic] relationship, so why did I feel like I was drowning in it? ... I realized that I had been attempting to fit myself into a mold that didn't fit because I was trying to be someone I wasn't in order to please this other person. I knew that if I stayed in that relationship, I could never grow into the person I was meant to be."

This passage demonstrates how unhealthy relationships can prevent us from realizing our full potential and moving forward with our lives. In this instance, Gilbert comes to the realization that she has been trying to change herself in order to conform to the expectations of another person. As a result, she could not remain authentic and pursue the goals and dreams that were uniquely hers.

In a later part of the book, Gilbert makes the decision to end the unhealthy relationship so that she can concentrate on her own personal development and self-discovery. She develops the ability to accept her authentic self and to pursue the activities and pursuits that bring her the most happiness and satisfaction because of going through this process.

Overall, "Eat, Pray, Love" is a potent reminder of how important it is to identify the unhealthy relationships in our lives that are preventing us from realizing our full potential and then letting go of those unhealthy relationships. It is essential to be aware that not every connection will immediately result in either personal development or benefit to the individual. It takes time and effort to build meaningful relationships, and the benefits aren't always immediately apparent once they've been achieved. On the other hand, if you consistently put in the effort to nurture a connection but find that it does not result in any positive growth or benefits, it may be time for you to move on to something else. Trust your instincts and prioritize your own well-being when making decisions about whom to invest your time and energy into.

It is definitely very difficult to let your connection go. But when you have to think about your own personal growth, you need to motivate your connections. However, when they are not giving you anything positive, do not let them give you anything negative as well. Remember that your time and energy are valuable resources, so it's important to invest them wisely.

According to findings from studies conducted in psychology, being in an unhealthy relationship can have a significant negative effect on both our mental health and overall well-being. Exposure to negative social interactions, such as criticism, conflict, and invalidation, can lead to increased symptoms of depression, anxiety, and stress, according to research that was published in the Journal of Social and Personal Relationships in 2014. The study was conducted in 2014. In addition, a study that was conducted in 2017 and published in the Journal of Personality and Social Psychology found that people who were involved in toxic relationships were more likely to experience symptoms of anxiety and depression, as well as physical health problems such as headaches and stomach issues. This was found to be the case even though the study was conducted on people who were not involved in toxic relationships. The findings of these studies shed light on how unhealthy relationships can influence our mental and physical health, which can stifle our capacity for personal growth and advancement. When we are continually forced to deal with negativity and conflict in our relationships, it's difficult to concentrate on our own objectives and the objectives that we have set for ourselves. On the other hand, studies have shown that having supportive relationships and engaging in healthy social interactions can have a positive impact on both our mental and physical health. Inflammation is linked to a wide range of health issues, and a study that was conducted in 2013 and published in the Journal of Personality and Social Psychology discovered that people who had more supportive social interactions had lower levels of inflammation. This suggests that building and maintaining strong social connections can not only improve our overall well-being but also reduce the risk of developing chronic illnesses associated with inflammation. Therefore, it is important to prioritize social connections and make time for meaningful interactions with loved ones.

> ***"The less you associate with some people, the more your life will improve. Any time you tolerate mediocrity in others, it increases your mediocrity. An important attribute in successful people is their impatience with negative thinking and negative acting people."***
>
> *– Colin Powell*

4

THE COST OF CONSTANT CONNECTION: NAVIGATING THE FINE LINE BETWEEN EFFICIENCY AND BURNOUT IN THE DIGITAL AGE

Naveen was a prosperous businessman who had built his empire by putting in a lot of effort, committing a lot of time, and having a good understanding of the market. On the other hand, he suffered from a fatal flaw—an addiction to social media. Naveen took every opportunity to brag about his success and wealth on his various social media accounts. He posted pictures of his extravagant lifestyle, including his expensive cars and his travels to far-off lands. He took pleasure in the attention and validation he received from the people who followed him online. But as time went on, Naveen's dependence on his addiction to social media became more and more overwhelming for him. He wasted a lot of time scrolling through his feed and kept checking back to see if there were any new comments or likes. At first, Naveen's company continued to enjoy a lot of success. Because of his presence on social media, he gained new customers and investors, and as a result, he was making more money than he ever had before. However, as time passed, Naveen realized that his success was not sustainable and that he needed to focus on building a strong foundation for his company to ensure long-term growth and profitability. But till then he was addicted.

His work started to suffer as his addiction got worse. He

missed critical deadlines, made poor decisions for the company, and ignored the needs of his employees. His preoccupation with social media had clouded his judgment, and it had led him down a path that could have potentially dangerous consequences. Naveen continued to post online despite the fact that his business was suffering. He couldn't abide the idea of losing his online fame and status, and it made him physically ill. He continued to put a strain on his financial situation by flaunting to his followers the ever more expensive possessions that he had purchased with his hard-earned money.

Naveen awoke one morning to discover that his various online accounts had been compromised by hackers. His followers had been posting critical comments and exposing the poor management of his finances. His reputation was ruined, and he had thrown away everything he had laboriously built over the course of his life. His addiction to social media had caused him to lose his business, as well as his reputation and his ability to provide for himself financially. Naveen concluded that his addiction to social media was a fruitless pursuit. He had been searching for fleeting and ultimately meaningless validation and attention all along, but he had not found it. He made a solemn vow to start over, devoting his attention to the quality of his personal and professional connections while turning his back on the destructive environment of social media.

The digital age has brought about a world of convenience and possibility, with technology making it easier than ever to stay connected to the world around us. But with the increase in our online interactions comes the potential for increased stress and anxiety, as well as a greater risk of burnout. As more of us find ourselves living our lives through our phones and computer screens, it is becoming increasingly important to take steps to ensure that we don't become overwhelmed by too much digital interaction.

One example of how people can become burned out by their online presence is through the phenomenon of "over-sharing". This occurs when individuals feel obligated to share every detail of their lives on social media, from what they had for breakfast to the latest news in their personal lives. While it is understandable to want to stay connected with friends and family, constantly updating your status or posting pictures can quickly become draining. It can also lead to feelings of anxiety and insecurity if you don't receive enough likes or comments on your posts.

Another way that people can be burned out by their online presence is through too much work-related communication. As more companies move towards remote working arrangements, employees are increasingly expected to be available at all times via email and other digital platforms. This can lead to a feeling of being constantly "on call" which can be mentally exhausting and create a sense of pressure that makes it difficult to relax and enjoy life outside of work hours.

Finally, another way in which people may become burned out by their online presence is through the constant need for comparison with others. Social media has made it incredibly easy to compare our own lives with those we see around us, creating unhealthy levels of competition where we continually strive for perfection rather than enjoying the moment as it comes. This can lead to feelings of inadequacy and low self-esteem if one does not measure up in terms of success or looks according to societal standards.

HOW CRUEL CAN SOCIAL MEDIA BECOME FOR YOU IF NOT KEPT UNDER CHECK?

The digital age has brought about a world of convenience and possibility, with technology making it easier than ever to stay connected to the world around us. But with the increase in our online interactions comes the potential for increased stress and anxiety, as well as a greater risk of burnout.

Some may feel compelled to constantly check their social media accounts, while others may feel the need to keep up with the ever-changing world of politics and business. This constant need to stay up-to-date can be both mentally and physically exhausting.

The digital world has also created a culture of comparison, in which individuals are constantly trying to measure up to the standards set by others. This can lead to feelings of inadequacy and low self-esteem, as well as an increase in anxiety and depression.

The pressure to stay connected online can take an extreme toll on one's mental well-being. Constantly checking emails, monitoring social media accounts, and keeping up with the latest news is mentally draining and can lead to feelings of anxiety or stress. Furthermore, if someone feels obligated to constantly post updates and photos, they may become overwhelmed by their own presence online, leading to a decrease in productivity or even burnout.

Besides the mental effects associated with digital burnout, there are also physical health risks that come along with this type of lifestyle. Prolonged use of technology can lead to increased fatigue because of lack of sleep or exercise; headaches from staring at screens for too long; neck strain from poor posture; carpal tunnel syndrome from typing too much; and vision problems from over-exposure to blue light emitted by electronic devices such as phones and laptops. All these physical issues can compound on one another and ultimately have an adverse effect on overall health if not addressed.

In his book "Digital Minimalism", Cal Newport examines the concept of striking a balance between the benefits of technology and the need for connection, as well as the potential drawbacks of constant connection, such as burnout and distraction. Newport believes that this can be accomplished by practicing "digital minimalism". He promotes the idea of a "digital declutter", in which we disconnect from our electronic devices and evaluate the things that really contribute to the quality of our lives. Newport argues that the constant use of technology has led to a decrease in our ability to focus and be productive. He suggests that by taking intentional breaks from technology, we can improve our mental clarity and ultimately lead more fulfilling lives. His theories are widely taught when we talk about using the digital imprint of our life. Through his research, he has highlighted the importance of balancing our use of technology with face-to-face communication and introspection.

This is related to the concept that is discussed in the article "The Cost of Constant Connection". While the internet and other forms of technology have significantly improved how we work and communicate, their use can also result in feelings of exhaustion and a lack of concentration. These negative effects are often referred to as "digital burnout" or "techno stress" and can have a detrimental impact on our mental health and overall well-being. It is important to be mindful of our technology use and take breaks when necessary to prevent these negative consequences.

"Digital sabbaths" are a good illustration of this concept. During "digital sabbaths", people take a break from their technological devices for a set amount of time, such as over the course of a weekend. This frees up mental space and allows us to rejuvenate, both of which can lead to increased levels of both productivity and creativity. Digital sabbaths have become increasingly popular as people recognize the importance of disconnecting from technology and allowing themselves to fully engage in other activities. By doing so, individuals can also improve their mental health and reduce stress levels.

In the end, the most important thing is to find a balance that is appropriate for each of us as individuals. It is important to be aware of the potential drawbacks of technology and to take steps to mitigate them, despite the fact that technology can be of tremendous benefit.

SET BOUNDARIES AND BE CLEAR ABOUT HOW MUCH IS TOO MUCH!

The author Stephen Covey writes in his book "The 7 Habits of Highly Effective People" that the most important thing is not to prioritize what's on your schedule but to schedule your priorities. This emphasizes the significance of establishing limits for ourselves and placing a higher priority on those things that really matter in our lives. Covey's philosophy encourages individuals to focus on their values and goals rather than being consumed by the demands of others. By prioritizing our priorities, we can achieve a greater sense of purpose and fulfillment in our personal and professional lives.

When it comes to social media, it is easy to become engrossed in the never-ending scroll and lose track of the passage of time. It is addictive, and many of us are slaves to this addiction. The constant need for validation and the fear of missing out (FOMO) can further exacerbate this addiction, leading to negative effects on mental health and productivity.

FOMO is used to describe the feeling of anxiety that occurs when we think we are missing out on something exciting or important that is happening in the digital world. This feeling is often compounded because it seems like everyone else is having a great time and we can't keep up. This can lead to feelings of inferiority, jealousy and insecurity, which can take a toll on our mental health. It can also cause us to become obsessed with always being in the know, which can lead to us neglecting our own lives and needs.

On the other hand, if we make other aspects of our lives a higher priority, like our health, our relationships, and our work, we will be better able to manage the time we spend on social media. In addition, author Cal Newport states in his book "Deep Work" that ***"the ability to concentrate intensely is a skill that must be trained".*** It is important to set aside specific times for social media use and to limit the amount of time spent on these platforms in order to improve our ability to concentrate and engage in deep work. Additionally, practicing mindfulness techniques such as meditation can also aid in improving our ability to focus. Putting limits on how much time we spend on social media can help us improve our ability to concentrate and pay attention to the activities and concerns that really matter in our lives, which increases productivity, creativity, and all-round well-being.

It is essential to establish boundaries when it comes to the use of social media and be aware of how much is too much of a good thing. We can find a balance that works for us and lead a life that is more fulfilling if we train our ability to concentrate and focus and put what is truly important at the top of our priority list.

DIGITAL DETOX – A NEW VOGUE

Detoxing from digital devices has become popular among celebrities, and the practice has had a positive effect not only on them but also on those around them. For instance, singer Ed Sheeran announced in 2019 that he would be taking a hiatus from social media and email for the next 18 months, citing the "toxic" nature of both platforms. Besides this, he did not have a phone for a period of time and relied solely on a flip phone to communicate via voice calls and text messages. This decision allowed him to focus on his mental health and personal relationships, as well as to avoid the distractions that come with being constantly connected. Sheeran's break from technology highlights the growing concern over the negative effects of social media and the need for individuals to disconnect and prioritize their well-being.

Emma Watson disclosed in an interview that she has taken extended breaks from social media, stating that she found it to be "overwhelming" and that it contributed to her anxiety. Besides this, she emphasized the significance of practicing mindfulness in relation to the use of technology and social media. She also discussed the impact of social media on mental health and suggested ways to limit screen time to maintain a healthy balance between online and offline activities.

Jennifer Aniston disclosed in an interview that she had taken a month-long break from social media in order to "detox" and recharge in 2018. Besides this, she emphasized the significance of disconnecting from technology in order to concentrate on one's own health and well-being.

The founder of the Huffington Post and author of the book "The Sleep Revolution," Arianna Huffington, has been a vocal advocate for digital detoxes and the importance of unplugging from technology. Her book is titled "The Sleep Revolution." She has shared in public about her own struggles with burnout and the positive effects that taking breaks from technology has had on her life.

Tanya Goodin delves into the topic of digital detoxes and how they can enhance one's life in her book "Off: Your Digital Detox for a Better Life." In the book, Goodin makes the argument that our constant connection to technology is one factor that is contributing to feelings of stress, anxiety, and burnout and that taking breaks from technology can be an effective way to improve our mental health and overall well-being. Goodin provides practical tips and advice on how to successfully disconnect from technology, including setting boundaries, finding alternative activities, and creating a support system. She also emphasizes the importance of being mindful and intentional about our use of technology in order to achieve a healthier balance in our lives. A digital detox can be accomplished by following the advice and methods provided by Goodin, which include establishing goals and limits for one's use of technology, seeking out alternative activities to replace digital distractions, and engaging in mindfulness practices in order to remain fully present in the here and now. She also provides real-life examples of people who have participated in digital detoxes and the positive effects that they have experienced as a result, such as improved sleep, decreased stress, and increased creativity. Overall, Goodin's approach to digital detox emphasizes the importance of being intentional and mindful in our use of technology and highlights the potential benefits of taking a break from constant digital stimulation. By following her advice, individuals can cultivate a healthier relationship with technology and improve their overall well-being.

"Off" presents an interesting argument for the benefits of digital detoxes for anyone looking to unplug and find a better balance between real life and their digital lives.

'IF WE ARE READY TO STEP BACK A LITTLE, SOCIAL MEDIA CAN BE A BLISS'

To be fair, not everything about social media is negative. Permit me to illustrate this with a current event taken from my life. My mother had a friend when she was in college, but after she got married, they fell out of touch with one another. The next day, suddenly, she sees her friend in her dream, and the day after that, she gets excited. She decides to reach out to her friend and reconnect with her after all these years, hoping that they can catch up on each other's lives and rekindle their friendship. She wonders if it was just a coincidence or if there was something more to the dream she had. She is eager to renew her relationship with her friend. I was the one who came up with the idea that we could look for her on the Internet given that we knew where she had gotten married. After conducting extensive research for about a quarter of an hour, I could locate my mother's high school friend and the two of them relived the days of their college life together. It was heartwarming to see my mother reconnect with her long-lost friend, and it made me realize the power of technology in bringing people together even after decades of separation. I hope to continue using this tool to help others reunite with their loved ones as well.

The power of social media can be seen in this example. But that is not the end of it. If you keep a time limit on it, you will also reap the benefits of many other potential advantages. For example, the use of social media can be extremely distracting, diverting our attention away from necessary activities and desired outcomes. If we reduce the amount of time, we spend on social media, we will be better able to concentrate on the things that really matter, whether that be our jobs, personal endeavours, or hobbies. Using social media less frequently has been shown to improve our overall mental health and reduce our vulnerability to the negative effects of social media. It is important to prioritize face-to-face interactions and engage in activities that promote well-being, such as exercise and mindfulness practices. Additionally, setting boundaries and limiting exposure to triggering content can also contribute to a healthier relationship with social media.

Although social media platforms make it simple to connect with many individuals, the quality of these relationships is frequently superficial and devoid of genuine intimacy. By reducing the amount of time we spend on social media, we will free up mental space to concentrate on developing deeper, more meaningful relationships with the people who are most important to us. This can lead to a greater sense of fulfillment and satisfaction in our personal lives. Additionally, it can improve our mental health by reducing the stress and anxiety that often come with constantly scrolling through social media feeds.

Creativity can be stifled by social media because it presents us with a constant stream of ideas and content generated by other people. However, increased creativity can result from using social media. By reducing the amount of time we spend on social media, we will free up more mental space for us to investigate our own thoughts and find creative ways to express ourselves. Moreover, social media can provide a platform for individuals to share their creative works and receive feedback from a wider audience, which can further enhance their creativity.

Social media has the potential to be an effective medium for self-expression; however, it also has the potential to be a fertile ground for competition and uncertainty about one's own abilities. We can cultivate a deeper sense of self-awareness and a more robust understanding of our own values and priorities if we reduce the amount of time we spend on social media. It is important to remember that social media only shows a curated version of people's lives, which can lead to unrealistic comparisons and feelings of inadequacy. By taking a step back from social media, we can focus on our own personal growth and development without the pressure of external validation.

5

THE SILENT PARTNER: HARNESSING THE POWER OF YOUR UNCONSCIOUS MIND

Spending some time by ourselves, getting lost in our own thoughts, and introspection is something that many of us do regularly. We are not necessarily feeling sad or depressed during these times; rather, we are having a conversation in our heads with the part of our mind that is not consciously aware of what is going on. When we give ourselves time to be by ourselves and to be quiet, we open the door for our subconscious mind to come to the surface. This allows our mind to provide us with insights, solutions, and creative ideas that we otherwise may not have had access to. The act of reflecting on one's own thoughts, feelings, and experiences can lead to greater self-awareness and comprehension of these aspects of one's life. Because of this, we may be better able to empathize with and comprehend the experiences of other people, as we will have gained a better understanding of the complexity and breadth of the human condition.

On the other hand, it is essential to keep in mind that prolonged periods of time spent alone can result in feelings of loneliness and disconnection from other people. It is essential that we find a balance between the time we spend engaging in self-reflection and the time we spend participating in social activities that bring us closer to other people. This balance can be achieved by setting aside specific times for socializing and trying to maintain relationships with friends and family.

Additionally, participating in group activities or volunteering can provide opportunities for both self-reflection and social connection. Taking the time to sit quietly by ourselves with our thoughts is a beneficial practice that can assist us in gaining clarity and insight into our own lives. We can learn to embrace the art of solitude and use it to enhance both our personal development and our well-being if we first gain an understanding of the power that our subconscious mind possesses.

THE POWER THAT WE POSSESS BUT NEVER EXPLORE

The power that resides in our subconscious mind is something that the majority of us fail to recognize or appreciate. It is the companion in the background that directs our choices and actions. In this chapter, we will discuss the power that lies within our subconscious and the ways in which we can harness that power to our benefit.

The subconscious, also known as the unconscious mind, is a region of the brain that regulates our reflexes. The limbic system—a region of the brain responsible for memory storage and retrieval, information processing, and emotion regulation—operates in the background to shape our choices without our knowledge.

The subconscious is a potent force that can be harnessed to assist us in accomplishing our objectives and realizing our ambitions. It is possible to use it to bring about positive changes in our lives and to assist us in making more informed decisions.

> ***"The silent partner within is the master strategist of your life, making moves in the grand chessboard of your mind."***

Imagine your mind as a vast chessboard, with each thought and decision represented by a piece on that board. You, the conscious thinker, are one of the players, but there's another player in this game, one who operates in silence, hidden in the shadows of your awareness. This silent partner within is the master strategist of your life.

As you go about your day, making choices and taking actions, it may seem like you're in control of every move.

You ponder your options, weigh the consequences, and make decisions based on your knowledge and experience. But beneath the surface, in the depths of your unconscious mind, the silent partner is at work.

This silent partner is a formidable strategist, always several steps ahead. It anticipates your desires, understands your fears, and navigates the intricate labyrinth of your emotions. It's as if this inner strategist has been playing the game of life for far longer than you have, and it has an innate understanding of the rules.

Sometimes, you may feel a sudden intuition—a gut feeling that guides you in a certain direction. It's as if a hidden hand moved a chess piece on the board of your mind, setting you on a course you didn't consciously plan. That's the silent partner making its move.

Consider those moments when you've had a brilliant idea seemingly out of nowhere or when a solution to a complex problem suddenly crystallized in your mind during a mundane activity like taking a shower or going for a walk. That's the silent partner's strategic brilliance at work.

The silent partner doesn't communicate through words or thoughts you can readily access. Instead, it communicates through feelings, hunches, and that inner voice that sometimes whispers softly in your ear. It's the source of your creativity, your intuition, and your ability to make leaps of faith.

To harness the power of this silent partner, you must learn to trust it. Understand that it has your best interests at heart, and it's constantly working to move you toward your goals and aspirations.

But like any chess player, it requires your participation and cooperation. You must be willing to listen to its subtle cues and act upon them.

Life's grand chessboard is complex and ever-changing, but with the silent partner as your master strategist, you have a powerful ally. Together, you can navigate the challenges and opportunities that come your way, making moves that lead you toward a more fulfilling and purposeful existence. So, the next time you feel that inner nudge or hear that quiet whisper, remember that it's your silent partner guiding you on the grand chessboard of your life.

> ***'Our subconscious mind emerges when we take time to be alone and quiet.'***

Visualization is one method that can be used to access the power that the subconscious has to offer. When we engage in visualization, we conjure up mental images of the goals we want to accomplish and the results we want to see. Imagining the result we want to achieve is a powerful way to communicate with our subconscious and let it know that this is something we care deeply about achieving.

Affirmations are statements that we make to ourselves in a positive manner with the intention of reprogramming our subconscious minds. They can be utilized to assist us in becoming more optimistic and focusing on our objectives.

The power of our subconscious mind can also be accessed by us through the practice of meditation. Meditation is a powerful method that allows us to connect with the desires and thoughts that lie dormant within us.

When we meditate, we open up a channel to our subconscious mind and strengthen the connection we have with it. This connection can be used to assist us in gaining insight into our own behaviors and what drives us to do the things that we do.

We have the power to bring about positive changes in our lives and accomplish what we set out to do by employing techniques such as visualization, affirmations, meditation, and hypnosis. And these are just some of the many ways that we can put the power of our subconscious mind to work for us.

We can tap into the power of our subconscious mind and put it to work for us to bring about positive changes in our lives if we practice hypnosis, meditation, positive self- talk, and other similar techniques. The power of the subconscious mind is a partner in disguise that can assist us in achieving our objectives and making our dreams come true.

THE PECULIAR STORY OF EDWIN BARNES

The book "Think and Grow Rich" by Napoleon Hill is credited with providing one of the most famous illustrations of the power that lies within the subconscious mind. In the book, Hill tells the story of a man named Edwin Barnes who had an intense yearning to collaborate with Thomas Edison but was never given the opportunity to do so.

Barnes was lacking in both connections and experience, but he was confident in his ability to achieve success through his collaboration with Edison. Therefore, he embarked on a journey to New Jersey in order to speak with Edison about obtaining employment there. After he arrived, the receptionist informed him that there were no vacancies at the moment.

Barnes, on the other hand, was not discouraged. He made the decision to remain in New Jersey and proceed with the pursuit of his objective. He found work in the area and made it a routine to stop by Edison's laboratory daily, where he introduced himself and stated that he was interested in collaborating with Edison.

Months passed, and Barnes was no closer to receiving an offer of employment. Despite this, he persisted in his efforts and refused to give up on achieving his objective. Edison gave Barnes an opportunity to work for him when he finally took notice of Barnes' dogged determination one day. After that, Barnes would go on to become one of Edison's most reliable and prosperous business associates. The life of Edwin Barnes serves as a powerful example of the ability of the subconscious mind to guide us toward the accomplishment of our objectives. Barnes could tap into the power of his subconscious mind and turn his dream into reality by having an intense desire and unwavering faith in his capacity to collaborate with Edison.

"Listen closely to the silent partner within, for it speaks the language of your deepest desires and aspirations."

But imagine your deepest desires and aspirations as a hidden treasure buried within your consciousness. These desires can be related to your career, relationships, personal growth, or any other aspect of your life. They often lie beneath the surface, obscured by the noise and distractions of daily life.

The conscious mind, the part of you that thinks and makes decisions daily, sometimes struggles to fully understand, or access these deep desires. It may be clouded by doubt, fear, or external influences. This is where the silent partner comes into play.

The silent partner is like a bridge between your conscious mind and your innermost desires. It has a direct line to your heart's truest wishes. When you learn to listen closely to it, you tap into a spring of guidance and insight.

This silent partner doesn't speak in sentences or articulate thoughts like your conscious mind. Instead, it communicates through a subtle symphony of emotions, instincts, and sensations.

To listen closely to your silent partner, you must cultivate self-awareness and mindfulness. Pay attention to your inner feelings and intuitions. Notice when something resonates with you on a profound level, even if you can't explain it logically. These are the whispers of your silent partner.

Trust in the wisdom of this silent partner. It knows what truly fulfills you, what ignites your passion, and what brings you closer to your aspirations. By tuning into this subtle but powerful source of guidance, you can make choices and take actions that align with your deepest desires, ultimately leading to a more authentic and fulfilling life.

So, listen closely to the silent partner within, for it speaks the language of your most cherished dreams and aspirations, guiding you toward a life that resonates with your heart's truest desires.

THE ART OF SOLITUDE: EMBRACING THE POWER OF INTROSPECTION

The practice of finding peace and clarity through introspection and reflection is an important part of the art of solitude. It is an effective practice that has the potential to bring about increased self-awareness and personal development. A great number of well-known figures recognize the value of time spent alone as a tool for advancing their careers and fostering their creative abilities.

One well-known example of this is the author JK Rowling, who is rumored to have written the first Harry Potter book while she was by herself in a coffee shop in Edinburgh, Scotland. Rowling was a single mother struggling with depression at the time she wrote "Harry Potter and the Sorcerer's Stone".

Rowling has addressed the public on numerous occasions regarding the significance of solitude, stating, ***"It is challenging to be creative in a world that is full of noise. The best companion for***

creative work is quiet isolation." Spending time by herself allowed her to access her subconscious mind and her most private thoughts and feelings, which ultimately resulted in the production of one of the most commercially successful book series in the history of publishing.

In a similar vein, the German philosopher Friedrich Nietzsche is yet another well-known figure who recognized the value of spending time alone. Nietzsche was famous for his habit of spending extended periods of time in the mountains by himself, where he would meditate and consider his beliefs and philosophy. Some of his best-known works, such as "Thus Spoke Zarathustra" and "Beyond Good and Evil," were written by him during these times when he was by himself.

Nietzsche believed that an individual could develop a deeper understanding of both themselves and the world in which they found themselves by confronting their own thoughts and feelings when they were alone.

> ***"The more you spend time with yourself, the more you get to know about the world around you."***

Henry David Thoreau, an American author, and philosopher is credited with having written one of the best-known stories about the transformative effects of living alone for an extended period of time. Thoreau spent two years living alone in a cabin close to Walden Pond in Massachusetts and wrote extensively about his time spent by himself and the significance of making time to be alone with one's own thoughts.

Thoreau famously wrote: ***"I never found the companion that was so companionable as solitude."***

Thoreau believed that spending time alone was the best way to reacquaint oneself with oneself and the natural world because it removed one from the distractions and noise of society. He was of the opinion that one could improve their understanding of both themselves and the world around them by spending time by themselves in natural settings.

In a similar vein, the musician and artist David Bowie recognized the value of seclusion as an essential component of his creative process. Bowie was well known for his tendency to spend extended periods of time by himself, during which he explored his artistic vision and experimented with a variety of musical styles. He once said, ***"I'm quite an introspective person, and I need that alone time to recharge my batteries."***

Spending time alone can be an effective method of recharging and rejuvenating oneself on a creative as well as an emotional level. We can achieve a greater sense of personal fulfillment and purpose in our lives by cultivating moments of introspection in which we can access our most private thoughts and feelings, as well as find moments of peace and clarity. Taking time for oneself can also help in reducing stress and anxiety, and can lead to a better understanding of one's own needs and desires, which can ultimately lead to a more fulfilling life.

Numerous powerful people throughout history have argued in favor of the importance of spending time by yourself. We can improve our understanding of ourselves and the world around us, as well as our personal development and sense of fulfilment if we make the effort to spend some time alone with our thoughts regularly.

One famous story that illustrates how being alone can activate the unconscious mind and lead to success is the story of Isaac Newton and the apple. As the story goes, Newton was sitting under an apple tree, lost in thought, when an apple fell from the tree and hit him on the head. This experience led him to develop his theory of gravity, one of the most important scientific discoveries in history.

While the story may be somewhat apocryphal, it is often cited as an example of how moments of solitude and introspection can spark creative insights and new ideas. Newton was known for spending a great deal of time alone, and he once wrote, "***I do not know what I may appear to the world, but to myself, I seem to have been only like a boy playing on the seashore, and diverting myself in now and then finding a smoother pebble or a prettier shell than ordinary, whilst the great ocean of truth lay all undiscovered before me.***"

The story of the apple serves as a powerful reminder of the importance of taking time to be alone with our thoughts, and the potential for great insights and discoveries that can arise from such moments.

Furthermore, the benefits of solitude and introspection are not limited to scientific discoveries or creative insights. In fact, many successful leaders and entrepreneurs attribute their success to their ability to spend time alone and reflect on their goals and strategies. For example, Steve Jobs was known for taking long walks alone to clear his mind and generate new ideas for Apple. Similarly, Warren Buffett has credited his success to his ability to spend hours alone reading and thinking about investments. These examples demonstrate that solitude and introspection can be powerful tools for achieving success in a variety of fields.

> ***"Your unconscious mind is the silent architect of your reality, shaping your world one thought at a time."***

In a small village nestled among the lush green hills of southern India, there lived a young man named Arjun. Arjun was an aspiring artist known for his intricate, colorful paintings that seemed to capture the soul of the village. Yet, he had dreams of becoming a renowned artist known throughout the world.

Arjun's journey toward realizing his dreams began with a single thought, a vision he couldn't shake from his mind's eye. He saw himself standing on a grand stage, his artwork adorning the walls of prestigious galleries, and people from distant lands admiring his creations. It was a dream that stirred his soul and filled his heart with an unquenchable fire.

But there was a challenge. Arjun lived in a modest village, and the prospect of making a name for himself in the competitive world of art seemed distant and unattainable. Doubt crept into his conscious mind, and he questioned whether his dream was just a fantasy.

Yet, there was a silent architect at work within Arjun the unconscious mind. Every day, as he painted the scenes of his village and its people, he poured his passion and unwavering belief into his artwork. He immersed himself in the creative process, losing track of time as his thoughts flowed effortlessly onto the canvas.

One evening, as the sun dipped below the horizon, Arjun unveiled his latest masterpiece—a vibrant depiction of his dream. It was an image of him standing on that grand stage, surrounded by art enthusiasts and critics, his paintings basking in the spotlight. The unconscious mind had guided his hand, and the painting felt like a piece of his soul captured on canvas.

The villagers gathered around, marveling at the painting's beauty. They could feel the determination and the dreams within it. Arjun's work began to attract attention, not just from the villagers but also from art collectors who traveled from the city to witness his talent.

Word of Arjun's remarkable artwork soon reached the city's art community. His paintings were displayed in a nearby gallery, and he was invited to showcase his work at an art exhibition in the bustling city. Slowly but steadily, his dreams were manifesting into reality, one thought at a time.

As Arjun continued to paint with passion and dedication, his unconscious mind remained the silent architect, shaping his world according to his visions. With each stroke of his brush, he moved closer to the grand stage he had envisioned, ultimately becoming the renowned artist he had dreamt of becoming.

This story illustrates how our unconscious mind can be the silent architect of our reality.

BEING AN INTROVERT CAN BE A VIRTUE

"Quiet: The Power of Introverts in a World That Can't Stop Talking" by Susan Cain is an excellent example of a book that investigates how spending time by oneself can stimulate the unconscious mind and lead to accomplishments. In the book, Cain makes the argument that introverts, who are people who typically enjoy spending time by themselves, frequently have a special ability to connect with their unconscious minds, which can lead to creative and innovative thinking.

Cain observes that a number of the most successful artists, writers, and thinkers in the history of the world have been introverts who spent a significant amount of time by themselves. She talks about how author JK Rowling spent years writing the first Harry Potter book in cafes and on trains while her baby daughter slept, and she talks about how scientist Albert Einstein was known for taking long walks alone to think and reflect.

Cain also notes that introverts often have a strong capacity for deep thinking and introspection, which can help them better understand their own motivations and goals. She contends that cultivating this self-awareness can pave the way for greater success and fulfilment in one's life.

Overall, "Quiet" presents a convincing argument for the power of introverts and the significance of making time to be by oneself, which is an important theme throughout the film. The author of the book proposes that by embracing our natural inclinations toward introversion and solitude, we can engage our unconscious minds and access our greatest potential for achievement and creativity.

'ME TIME, ALONE TIME'

The following passage from Maya Angelou beautifully expresses the significance of spending time by oneself:

"Every person needs to take one day away. A day in which one consciously separates the past from the future. Jobs, family, employers, and friends can exist one day without any of us, and if our egos permit us to confess, they could exist eternally in our absence. Each person deserves a day away in which no problems are confronted, and no solutions searched for. Each of us needs to withdraw from the cares which will not withdraw from us."

It is essential to keep in mind that everyone has their own preferences when it comes to the ratio of time spent alone to time spent with other people. When it comes to these preferences, there is no "right" or "wrong" way to approach them as long as we are taking care of our own requirements and maintaining our well-being. It is important to recognize and respect our own individual needs for solitude or socialization, and not feel pressured to conform to societal expectations. Ultimately, finding a balance that works for us is key to living a fulfilling life.

According to the findings of a study that was published in the Journal of Personality and Social Psychology, spending time alone has the potential to boost our levels of creativity and productivity, as well as our mood and our overall health. Another study that was published in the Journal of Environmental Psychology discovered that spending time alone in natural settings can improve cognitive functioning and reduce stress.

In a similar vein, a study that was recently published in the Journal of Applied Social Psychology discovered that introverts, who are people who prefer to spend time by themselves, are more likely to have higher levels of both creativity and achievement. In addition, studies on mindfulness meditation have shown that spending some time alone with one's thoughts can improve our ability to concentrate, help us better control our feelings, and lessen our levels of anxiety and stress.

These studies suggest that taking time for oneself can have a positive impact on our creativity, productivity, mood, and overall well-being. Moreover, incorporating mindfulness meditation into our daily routine can also enhance our relationships with others by improving our communication skills and empathy toward others. Therefore, taking some time to practice mindfulness meditation can have far-reaching benefits for both our personal and professional lives.

If you like being alone, use it to pursue your interests, reflect on your feelings, and take care of yourself.

Scientific research has shown that spending time alone can enhance creativity, productivity, cognitive functioning, mood, and overall well-being. Whether we are introverted or extroverted, we all need time to ourselves in order to recharge and renew our energy and focus. So, if you enjoy being alone, embrace it and use it as an opportunity to explore your passions, reflect on your thoughts and emotions, and take care of yourself.

6

THE TENSION BETWEEN PROGRESS AND JUSTICE: NAVIGATING THE PATH TO A BETTER FUTURE

For decades, the city of Bhopal was a symbol of India's unstoppable industrial development. The nineteenth-century palace of Begum Shah Jahan and her beautiful garden at the center of the city had been transformed with such speed that it seemed as if an army of men had simply swept away everything that stood in their way. Between 1860, when the British East India Company made Bhopal its headquarters, and 1947, when India gained independence, the city grew from a small walled town to one of India's largest cities. Its rapid growth led many to call the city "the Manchester of the East."

In the 1960s and '70s, Bhopal moved even faster. Factories producing chemicals, pesticides, medicines, and other products sprang up on all sides. The population grew rapidly as people came from around Madhya Pradesh state to take advantage of economic opportunities in Bhopal. Increasing numbers of women joined the workforce in these factories; soon, there were more working women than anywhere else in India.

The expansion of the industry was good for jobs and for families with members employed by the factories. However, there were also growing concerns about social problems associated with new industries: pollution, health issues related to hazardous working conditions, housing shortages for the influx of migrants from the countryside, and labour unrest over low wages and poor working conditions.

In 1984, these concerns came to a tragic climax with the Bhopal gas tragedy, one of the worst industrial disasters in history. A gas leak at the Union Carbide pesticide plant in the city released toxic gas into the air, killing thousands of people and injuring many more. The tragedy highlighted the devastating human cost of unbridled industrial development and the need for greater attention to social justice and human rights in the pursuit of progress.

In the wake of the disaster, civil society organizations, non-governmental organizations, and local communities mobilized to demand better safety standards and increased accountability from corporations and the government. This activism had an impact: in 1989, the Supreme Court of India passed an order that established a framework for monitoring industrial pollution, overseeing occupational health and safety, and providing compensation for victims.

In recent years, India has become increasingly aware of the need for sustainable development that takes into account environmental, social, and economic concerns. The country has made progress in formulating policies to ensure responsible resource management; for example, it has launched the National Clean Air Programme, which sets long-term air quality standards for major cities across India. It has also taken steps to promote corporate social responsibility through legislation like the Companies Act 2013 which requires companies to contribute towards community welfare projects through their profits.

Despite these efforts, cases of industrial pollution continue to be reported across India. Moreover, rising urbanization is creating new challenges, such as traffic congestion, housing shortages, and inadequate waste management systems that cannot be addressed by traditional industrial policies alone. In order to meet this challenge, policymakers must take a holistic approach to urban planning that considers not only economic growth but also human rights and environmental protection.

As India moves forward on its path of development, it is important for all stakeholders—citizens, civil society organizations, businesses, and policymakers—to remain mindful of their responsibilities when it comes to protecting human rights and preserving our environment for future generations.

The Bhopal gas tragedy was a stark reminder of the difficult trade-offs that we sometimes face when trying to balance progress and justice. It raised important questions about the costs of industrial development, the responsibilities of corporations, and the role of government in regulating the industry and protecting the rights and welfare of citizens.

The tragedy had been an eye-opening experience for many people who had been complacent about the pursuit of progress. It had revealed a glaring lack of accountability and transparency and had caused many to question whether the price of progress was too high when it came to human lives and the environment.

The tragedy highlighted the need for more responsible and sustainable forms of progress that prioritize people and the environment as much as profits. It also motivated people to action. It spurred calls for greater oversight and more stringent regulations and sparked conversations about how to ensure equitable development that meets the needs of both people and the planet. In the wake of the tragedy, people everywhere were determined to make sure that such a disaster never happened again and to do whatever was necessary to guarantee that the pursuit of progress was done responsibly and sustainably.

THE TENSION OF PROGRESS VS JUSTICE

Since the beginning of civilization, people have struggled to find a way to balance the pursuit of progress with a commitment to justice. On the one hand, progress is responsible for increased economic growth, increased technological advancement, and an overall improvement in people's standard of living. On the other hand, if we are to adhere to the principles of justice, it is imperative that such progress not be accomplished at the expense of individuals and groups who are marginalized and oppressed. If humanity is going to make progress toward a better future, then this tension is one that needs to be worked through. It is essential to recognize the historical and systemic inequalities that have resulted in the oppression and marginalization of certain groups. We can never truly make progress that is to the benefit of everyone in society unless we address these issues. In this chapter, we will investigate how this tension presents itself, the strategies that can be utilized to address it, and the steps that can be taken to realize a brighter future.

> ***"The pursuit of progress often comes at a cost to justice, but the pursuit of justice need not come at a cost to progress."***
>
> ***– Henry Waxman,***
> ***Former US congressional representative***

When we prioritize progress—economic expansion or technological advancement—there is a possibility that it will have unintended consequences that will detrimentally affect justice, such as increased social inequality or deterioration of the natural environment.

On the other hand, the quote by Waxman seems to imply that it is possible to seek progress and justice simultaneously without having to make a choice between the two and sacrifice one for the other. For instance, policies and initiatives that prioritize environmental sustainability, social equity, and human rights can help to ensure that progress is achieved in a manner that is fair, just, and sustainable. This can help ensure that the goals of the policies and initiatives are met. Furthermore, the pursuit of justice can actually be a driver of progress because it can inspire new innovations, policies, and practices that promote greater social and environmental responsibility. This can be a very positive thing for society. If we make justice and progress our top priorities, we will create a future that is more equitable and sustainable for everyone.

To build a better future—characterized by sustained progress and prosperity for all—justice must be at the core of our efforts. Justice ensures that the benefits of progress are equitably distributed, that no one is left behind, and that societal structures are solid and enduring. It is the moral compass that guides us toward a future where progress and justice are not in conflict but are instead mutually reinforcing.

> ***"Progress without justice is like building a tower on shaky ground; it may rise high, but it's destined to fall. Let justice be the bedrock of our journey towards a better future."***

This thought-provoking statement encapsulates the fundamental relationship between progress and justice and underscores the critical role justice plays in sustaining long-term societal advancement.

Imagine progress as a towering structure—a symbol of human achievement, innovation, and development. In this analogy, each level of the tower represents a milestone of progress, whether it's technological advancements, economic growth, or social evolution. It's natural to focus on building the tower higher and higher, aspiring to reach new heights. However, the metaphorical tower's foundation often goes unnoticed, and that's where justice comes into play.

Justice is the bedrock upon which any society must build its progress. Just as a tower relies on a solid foundation to stand tall and withstand the test of time, progress depends on a foundation of justice to ensure its stability and longevity.

When a society prioritizes progress at the expense of justice, it may indeed experience rapid growth and development. However, this progress often masks deep rooted inequalities, discrimination, and injustices. It's akin to constructing a tower on unstable, shifting ground. For a while, it may seem impressive and towering, but over time, the inherent weaknesses in the foundation become apparent.

Without a commitment to justice, the tower of progress becomes increasingly unstable. The weight of unresolved grievances, disparities, and systemic injustices weakens the societal structure. Cracks begin to appear, and the tower's once-impressive height becomes a precarious liability. Eventually, it crumbles under the accumulated weight of injustice, leaving behind a trail of devastation and disillusionment.

To build a better future, one characterized by sustained progress and prosperity for all, justice must be at the core of our efforts. Justice ensures that the benefits of progress are equitably distributed, that no one is left behind, and that societal structures are solid and enduring.

THE ROLE OF POWER IN CREATING THE TENSION

"Power gives people the ability to achieve their goals, while powerlessness leaves people behind."

The unequal distribution of resources and power between the various actors is the root cause of the conflict that exists between progress and justice.

This dynamic is reflected in the current economic system, which is founded on unequal power and privilege for different groups of people. For instance, those who are wealthy have access to resources that those who are less fortunate do not, such as educational opportunities, financial capital, and various networks and resources.

> ***"Human progress is neither automatic nor inevitable... Every step toward the goal of justice requires sacrifice, suffering, and struggle; the tireless exertions and passionate concern of dedicated individuals."***
>
> ***– Martin Luther King Jr, Civil Rights Leader***

THE ROLE OF INEQUALITY IN CREATING THE TENSION

Another factor that contributes to the tension that exists between progress and justice is inequality. Those who hold power in a society where inequality is rampant can use that power to further their own interests, while those who are marginalized and oppressed cannot participate in the same way because of their position. This results in a situation in which justice is not served because it creates a situation in which progress is made at the expense of those who are already disadvantaged, and it creates a situation in which progress is made at the expense of those who are already disadvantaged.

The disparity in income that exists between those at the top of the income ladder and those at the bottom is one illustration of this phenomenon. Because those at the top have access to resources and opportunities that those at the bottom do not, a situation is created in which progress is made at the expense of justice, which ultimately results in increased inequality and injustice.

NAVIGATING THE PATH FOR A BETTER FUTURE

> ***"Justice cannot be for one side alone, but must be for both."***
>
> ***– Eleanor Roosevelt,***
> ***Former First Lady of the United States***

In order to build a better future, it is essential that the tension between progress and justice be navigated in a way that takes into account the needs of all individuals and groups. This requires a commitment to creating a fairer, more equitable society in which resources are shared, and power is distributed more evenly. This can be achieved through a variety of measures, such as:

1. **Addressing Inequality:** In order to reduce the tension between progress and justice, it is important to address the underlying inequality that creates it. This can be done through policies that address the underlying causes of inequality, such as poverty and a lack of education, and through targeted measures that help to level the playing field for those who are disadvantaged. Furthermore, it is crucial to ensure that these policies and measures are implemented in a way that does not further marginalize or discriminate against any group and that they are continuously evaluated and adjusted as needed to ensure their effectiveness in promoting both progress and justice.
2. **Investing in Education:** Investing in education can help create greater opportunity and access to resources for those who are disadvantaged, allowing them to participate in the economic system and achieve the same level of success as those who are more privileged. Furthermore, education can also lead to the development of critical thinking skills and the ability to make informed decisions,

which are essential for individuals to become active and engaged citizens in their communities. Investing in education is not only a moral imperative but also a smart economic decision.

3. **Supporting Marginalized Communities:** Supporting marginalized communities is essential for creating a fairer, more just society. This can be done through targeted measures, such as providing access to healthcare, education, and other resources, and by supporting organizations that seek to empower and advocate for those who are marginalized and oppressed. It is important to recognize that marginalized communities often face systemic barriers and discrimination that prevent them from accessing these resources. Therefore, it is crucial to address these underlying issues and work towards creating a more equitable society for all.

THERE'S STILL HOPE FOR JUSTICE

Vedanta Resources, a British mining company, made a proposal in 2003 to mine bauxite in the Niyamgiri hills, which are regarded as sacred by the indigenous Dongria Kondh tribe that lives in the area. Vedanta Resources has since withdrawn its proposal. The Dongria Kondh people opposed the mining project because they believed it would threaten their traditional way of life besides causing damage to their sacred lands. They also argued that the project would violate their rights under the Panchayat (Extension to Scheduled Areas Act) and the Forest Rights Act, both of which give indigenous communities greater control over their lands and resources. Both acts were passed in India.

The Vedanta mining project was initially approved by the Indian government; however, it was later canceled in 2014 by the

Supreme Court of India, which ruled that the project violated the rights of the indigenous Dongria Kondh tribe and posed a threat to the environment. The court stated that the project also posed a danger to the environment. The indigenous community's rights and interests were protected, and environmental sustainability was upheld because of the cancellation of the Vedanta mining project, which was seen as a victory for justice.

The project would have brought economic benefits to the region, including jobs and revenue, but the cancellation of the project was seen as a victory for justice. This case demonstrates that progress does not necessarily have to come at the expense of justice and that there are situations in which justice must take precedence over progress. Besides this, it emphasizes the significance of respecting the rights and interests of indigenous communities and promoting sustainable development that strikes a healthy balance between the needs of the economy, society, and the environment.

The case of the construction of the Keystone XL pipeline in the United States is another example of progress being sidelined because of justice. It was proposed that the pipeline would transport crude oil from Canada to the Gulf Coast. If built, the pipeline would have the potential to increase domestic energy production and create jobs.

However, the pipeline was met with fierce opposition from indigenous groups, environmental activists, and concerned citizens who argued that its construction would threaten the environment and violate the rights of indigenous communities. They argued that the pipeline would increase the risk of oil spills and contribute to climate change, which would have a disproportionate impact on vulnerable communities and future generations.

In 2015, the Obama administration courageously rejected the contentious Keystone XL Pipeline, which was celebrated by advocates of justice, as it both ensured the rights and interests of indigenous communities were respected and actively promoted sustainable development of energy sources that prioritize economic, social, and environmental compatibility.

The case of the Keystone XL Pipeline shows that progress can be achieved responsibly, without compromising justice. Besides recognizing the importance of justice, this example also highlights the need for governments to prioritize sustainable energy sources over conventional ones.

By rejecting the pipeline, President Obama showed his commitment to a future in which clean energy rather than fossil fuels dominates our economy. The decision was also commended by many environmental activists, who praised its emphasis on sustainability and responsibility towards future generations.

The conflict that arises from the conflicting goals of progress and justice is one that can be found throughout history and continues to be a source of difficulty for us today. It is essential in order to construct a better future that this tension be navigated in a way that takes into consideration the requirements of all the different individuals and groups involved. This necessitates a dedication to the creation of a society that is more just and equitable, in which resources are shared, and power is distributed more evenly to all members of society. We can get much closer to a better future in which both progress and justice are served if we tackle the problem of inequality, invest in education, and lend support to communities that are on the margins of society.

The debate between progress and justice is indeed complicated and multidimensional, and it involves a wide variety of issues and challenges that arise because of economic, social, and political advancement. However, progress may also have unintended consequences that have a detrimental effect on the administration of justice.

For instance, economic development has the potential to exacerbate existing social inequalities; technological progress has the potential to upend traditional ways of life and exacerbate existing environmental issues; and material prosperity has the potential to lead to the exploitation of natural resources and the degradation of the environment.

There are times when progress necessitates sacrificing justice in order to achieve its goals.

On the other hand, justice is frequently linked to concepts such as fairness, equality, and responsibility to one's community. It is motivated by the aspiration to establish a society that is more equitable and just, one in which every person has access to the fundamental rights and opportunities of the human race.

The pursuit of justice involves identifying and addressing the fundamental factors that contribute to social, economic, and environmental issues, as well as fostering social and environmental sustainability. However, justice can also be a barrier to progress because, in the short term, it can limit economic growth, technological advancement, and material prosperity. Justice can act as a brake on progress. For instance, policies that place a higher priority on social and environmental sustainability can be expensive and may call for significant investments in areas such as education, research and development, and infrastructure. This can reduce the resources that are available for other priorities, such as the expansion of the economy and the accumulation of material wealth. Finding a happy medium between these two competing values—progress and justice—is what will determine whether this conflict can be resolved.

This means acknowledging that progress and justice are not incompatible goals but ones that should be pursued in tandem. It means acknowledging that we need both progress and justice to create a society that is truly just and prosperous and that we need to pursue them in a way that is sustainable, equitable, and socially responsible. It also means that we need to acknowledge that we need to pursue them in a way that is socially responsible. This requires a shift in how we think about progress and development, as well as a greater emphasis on human rights, social responsibility, and environmental and social sustainability.

It also requires an increased level of collaboration between governments, corporations, and civil society, as well as a commitment to working together in order to address the complex challenges of our time. In conclusion, the argument regarding whether progress should be prioritized over justice is a convoluted and ongoing one that is relevant to a great deal of the most pressing problems of our era. However, if we acknowledge how these two principles are mutually supportive of one another and collaborate to find a middle ground between them, we will build a better and more equitable future not only for ourselves but also for future generations.

> ***"The ultimate test of a moral society is the kind of world that it leaves to its children."***
>
> ***– Dietrich Bonhoeffer, German Theologian***

This quote by Dietrich Bonhoeffer, a German theologian and pastor who lived during the Nazi regime, highlights the importance of a society's moral values and the impact they have on future generations. By taking action against injustices or embracing strategies to create more opportunities for others, we build a better world not only for ourselves but also for future generations.

Bonhoeffer experienced the Nazi regime first-hand, and he spoke openly against it, leading to his execution. He believed that the true measure of a moral society is the world it leaves for its children. The values and standards upheld by society will shape the world future generations are left with. If a society advocates for justice, empathy, and equity, then those traits will be passed on to generations to come. Conversely, if a nation values greediness, unfairness, and oppression, then those qualities will be seen in the world its children inherit.

A society should strive for justice, empathy, and equity so that its children inherit a world that is rooted in these values. If a society's principles center on selfishness, unfairness, and oppression, then those qualities will be seen in the world its children inherit. Ultimately, our actions today will shape the world tomorrow. We must take responsibility for our behavior and build an ethical legacy that gives our children the opportunity to live in a better world. We must be mindful of our actions and the impact they have on others if we are to achieve this goal. This is especially true when it comes to issues such as poverty, inequality, racism, sexism, and discrimination. Our actions today will determine the kind of world our children will inhabit tomorrow.

7

EGO VS. UNCONSCIOUSNESS: UNDERSTANDING THE BATTLE WITHIN

"The ego wants quantity; the soul wants quality."

- Wayne Dyer,

American self-help author and motivational speaker

("The Power of Intention")

In the depths of the human psyche lies an eternal struggle, a cosmic battle that shapes the very fabric of our existence—the clash between ego and unconsciousness. This primordial conflict, often obscured from conscious awareness, influences our thoughts, emotions, and actions. It is a duel that transcends time and culture, resonating through the ages as an enigmatic enigma of human experience.

At the heart of this struggle stands the ego, that ever-present sense of self, the center of our conscious awareness. The ego is the navigator of our waking life, guiding us through the labyrinth of reality and helping us make sense of the external world. It is the seat of our desires, ambitions, and insecurities, shaping our identities and coloring our perceptions. The ego is a formidable force, asserting itself with conviction and tenacity, striving to establish its dominance over the psyche.

Yet, lurking in the shadows of the conscious mind lies the enigmatic unconsciousness. An abyss of hidden desires, unresolved conflicts, and suppressed memories, the unconscious wields a mysterious power over the ego. Rooted in the depths of our being, the unconscious is an ancient repository of collective knowledge, carrying the echoes of our ancestors' experiences and wisdom. It is a realm of dreams, symbols, and archetypes, unfolding its cryptic messages in the nocturnal theater of the mind.

The battle between ego and unconsciousness is not a conflict of good and evil but a complex interplay of light and shadow. The ego, with its desire for control and self-preservation, often resists the revelations of the unconscious, fearing the chaos and vulnerability that lie within. It erects barriers, defense mechanisms, and denials to shield itself from the discomfort of self-awareness.

Consequently, the unconscious seeks expression through various channels, often manifesting in dreams, slips of the tongue, and unconscious biases. When repressed for too long, the unconscious can emerge in destructive ways, sabotaging relationships, causing emotional turmoil, and hindering personal growth. The more the ego suppresses the unconscious, the more potent and disruptive its influence becomes, like a dormant volcano waiting to erupt.

The path to enlightenment lies in recognizing this interplay and embracing the wisdom that the unconscious offers. The ego must acknowledge that it is not the sole architect of the self, but a fragment of a greater whole. In embracing the unconscious, we gain access to the hidden depths of our potential, unearthing dormant talents, unmasking hidden truths, and finding creative solutions to life's challenges.

Transcending the ego's resistance requires courage, humility, and a willingness to confront one's shadows. This confrontation is not an act of condemnation but a journey of integration and healing. As we venture into the depths of our unconscious, we unveil the wounds that shape our perceptions and behaviors, tenderly tending to them with self-compassion and understanding.

Philosophy and psychology converge in this battle between ego and unconsciousness, revealing the intrinsic connection between self-awareness and personal growth. It is a journey of individuation, where the fragmented self integrates into a harmonious whole, embracing both the light and darkness within.

In this union, we find a profound sense of authenticity, transcending the limitations of the ego and aligning with our true nature. The battle of ego and unconsciousness is not a conquest for dominance but an exploration of the human experience, a voyage that reveals the depth and complexity of the human soul.

As we embrace the mystery of this eternal struggle, we unlock the keys to a higher state of consciousness. It is a pilgrimage of self-discovery, a quest for truth and meaning in the vast expanse of existence. In the end, we come to realize that the battle between ego and unconsciousness is not a clash of adversaries but a dance of cosmic partners, forever entwined in the tapestry of human consciousness.

One of the most influential works on the subject of ego and unconsciousness comes from the renowned Swiss psychiatrist and psychoanalyst, Carl Gustav Jung, in his book "The Archetypes and the Collective Unconscious". In this seminal work, Jung delves into the depths of the human psyche, exploring the interplay between the ego and the unconscious mind.

Jung introduced the concept of the collective unconscious, which he believed was a repository of universal experiences and knowledge shared by all human beings. He posited that beyond the personal unconscious, which houses an individual's unique experiences and memories, there exists a deeper layer of the unconscious that contains the shared experiences of our ancestors and the collective wisdom of the human race.

The archetypes, according to Jung, are innate, universal symbols and patterns that reside in the collective unconscious.

These archetypes are manifestations of the fundamental human experiences, such as the Mother, the Father, the Hero, the Shadow, and more. They are found in myths, fairy tales, and religious stories across different cultures and time periods, reflecting the common threads that weave through humanity's psyche.

In Jung's view, the ego is the conscious self, the center of our waking awareness and the part of us that interacts with the external world. It develops through the process of individuation, where the individual separates from the collective unconscious and gains a sense of identity and autonomy.

However, the ego is not the entirety of the self. Jung argued that a complete understanding of oneself requires a deep exploration and integration of the contents of the unconscious, including the archetypes. He emphasized the importance of embracing the unconscious aspects of the psyche to achieve wholeness and self-realization.

The battle between the ego and the unconscious, according to Jung, is a struggle for balance and integration. The ego, with its emphasis on individuality and control, often resists the influence of the unconscious and the archetypes. It may dismiss or repress the messages and symbols emerging from the deeper layers of the psyche.

This resistance can lead to psychological and emotional conflicts, as well as a sense of emptiness or disconnection from the deeper layers of meaning in life. Jung believed that the process of individuation and self-discovery involves acknowledging and embracing the messages and insights offered by the unconscious, including the archetypes.

By engaging in this journey of self-awareness, individuals can gain profound insights into their own motivations, fears, and desires. They can recognize and confront their shadows—the darker and hidden aspects of their personality—and integrate them into a more balanced and harmonious self.

Jung's work on ego and unconsciousness continues to resonate with readers and scholars alike because it offers a framework for understanding the complexities of the human psyche. It provides a roadmap for personal growth and self-discovery, urging individuals to look within, confront their fears and limitations, and strive for a deeper understanding of themselves and their place in the collective tapestry of human experience. Through this process, Jung invites us to embrace the battle between ego and unconsciousness as a transformative journey that leads to a more authentic and meaningful life.

From a spiritual perspective, the struggle between ego and unconsciousness takes on a deeper significance, often viewed as a profound journey of self-realization and transcendence. Various spiritual traditions and teachings offer unique insights into this inner battle and its potential transformative power. Here are some key aspects of the spiritual perspective on the struggle between ego and unconsciousness:

1. **The Illusion of Ego:** Many spiritual philosophies consider the ego to be an illusion or a false sense of self. It is often seen as a construct that arises from identification with thoughts, emotions, and external circumstances. The ego creates a sense of separation and individuality, leading to desires, attachments, and a constant need for validation and control.
2. **The Awakening of Consciousness:** Spirituality invites individuals to awaken to a deeper level of consciousness beyond the ego. This awakening involves recognizing the limitations of the ego's narrow perspective and expanding one's awareness to connect with a higher,

more universal consciousness. It is becoming aware of the interconnectedness of all beings and the oneness of existence.

3. **Surrender and Letting Go:** Spiritual teachings often emphasize the importance of surrendering the ego's need for control and embracing a state of acceptance and letting go. By relinquishing attachment to outcomes and desires, individuals can open themselves to the flow of life and tap into the wisdom of the unconscious.
4. **Facing the Shadow:** Spirituality encourages individuals to confront and integrate their shadow aspects—the hidden and repressed parts of themselves, such as their fears, traumas, and unresolved emotions. By doing this, individuals can heal and transform these aspects, leading to a greater sense of wholeness and authenticity.
5. **Mindfulness and Self-Awareness:** Practices such as meditation and mindfulness are instrumental in developing self-awareness and observing the workings of the ego and unconscious mind. Through these practices, individuals can detach from identification with thoughts and emotions and gain insight into the deeper layers of their being.
6. **Transcendence and Unity Consciousness:** The ultimate goal of the spiritual journey is often described as a state of transcendence, where the individual moves beyond the confines of the ego and experiences a sense of unity consciousness. In this state, there is a profound recognition of the interconnectedness of all life and a dissolution of the boundaries that separate self from others.
7. **Service and Compassion:** As individuals progress on their spiritual path, they are called to shift their focus from self-centered desires to acts of service and compassion

towards others. By cultivating empathy and compassion, individuals align with the higher principles of the unconscious and contribute to the collective evolution of consciousness.

The spiritual perspective on the struggle between ego and unconsciousness involves recognizing the illusory nature of the ego, awakening to a higher level of consciousness, and embracing self-awareness and mindfulness. Through profound inner exploration, individuals can move closer to a state of spiritual fulfillment and authentic self-expression.

The struggle between ego and unconsciousness is also discussed by Eckhart Tolle, a renowned spiritual teacher and author in his book "The Power of Now".

Tolle explores the concept of ego and its impact on human consciousness. He emphasizes the importance of living in the present moment and transcending the influence of the ego, which he refers to as the "voice in the head". He suggests that the ego is a constant stream of thoughts, judgments, and self-referential narratives that create unnecessary suffering and distract individuals from experiencing the true essence of their being.

According to Tolle, the ego thrives on identifying with external possessions, achievements, and labels, leading to a false sense of identity. This identification with the egoic mind perpetuates a cycle of seeking happiness in future accomplishments or reminiscing about experiences, causing individuals to miss the richness and depth of the present moment.

Tolle's teachings align with the spiritual perspective on the struggle between ego and unconsciousness, as he advocates for self-awareness and mindful presence as a means to transcend the ego's grip on the mind. By observing the egoic thoughts without judgment and cultivating a state of non-resistance, individuals can dis-identify from the ego and connect with the consciousness that lies beyond it.

Through his teachings and books, Eckhart Tolle has become a leading voice in contemporary spirituality, inspiring countless individuals to embark on a journey of self-discovery and inner transformation. He encourages people to tap into the wisdom of the unconscious by quieting the noise of the ego and fully immersing themselves in the eternal now. This approach aligns with the spiritual quest to find inner peace, unity consciousness, and a deeper connection to the essence of life.

The solution to the struggle between ego and unconsciousness lies in fostering a harmonious relationship between the two aspects of the psyche and achieving a state of balance and integration. While it may not be a straightforward or quick fix, several practices and approaches can help individuals navigate this inner battle:

1. **Self-awareness and Mindfulness:** Cultivating self-awareness and practicing mindfulness are essential in becoming conscious of the ego's patterns, defense mechanisms, and unconscious influences. By observing the workings of the mind without judgment, individuals can develop a deeper understanding of their inner dynamics and recognize the ego's subtle influences.
2. **Inner Exploration and Integration:** Engaging in activities such as journaling, therapy, or self-reflection, can help uncover unconscious patterns and unresolved emotions. By facing and embracing the shadow aspects of the self, individuals can integrate these elements into their conscious awareness and find healing and wholeness.
3. **Letting Go of Attachments:** Recognizing and letting go of attachments to identity, outcomes, and material

possessions allows individuals to free themselves from the ego's constant need for validation and control.

4. **Surrender and Acceptance:** Practicing surrender and acceptance involves acknowledging the limitations of the ego and trusting in the flow of life. Letting go of the need to control every aspect of life can lead to a more profound sense of peace and alignment with the unfolding of the present moment.
5. **Compassion and Empathy:** Cultivating compassion and empathy towards oneself and others can soften the ego's rigidity and self-centeredness. By understanding the shared human experience and extending empathy to others, individuals can transcend the boundaries of the ego and connect on a deeper level.
6. **Spiritual Practices:** Engaging in spiritual practices, such as meditation, yoga, or contemplative prayer, can help individuals connect with a higher level of consciousness beyond the ego. These practices facilitate a direct experience of presence and unity, shifting the focus from egoic concerns to a more profound sense of interconnectedness.
7. **Humility and Gratitude:** Cultivating humility and gratitude can counteract the ego's tendency towards arrogance and entitlement. Recognizing and expressing gratitude for life's blessings fosters a sense of appreciation and humility, paving the way for a more authentic and meaningful existence.
8. **Seek Guidance:** Seeking guidance from wise mentors, spiritual teachers and learning from the experiences and wisdom of others can shed light on one's own journey of self-discovery and transformation.

> ***"The ego relies on the familiar. It is reluctant to experience the unknown, which is the very essence of life."***
>
> ***– Deepak Chopra,***
> ***Indian-American author and spiritual teacher,***
> ***The Book of Secrets***

The solution to the struggle between ego and unconscious-ness is not about eliminating the ego but integrating it into a broader, more conscious awareness. By undertaking this transformative journey, individuals can achieve a state of inner peace, authenticity, and alignment with their true nature.

One book that offers insights into the solution of the struggle between ego and unconsciousness is "A New Earth: Awakening to Your Life's Purpose" by Eckhart Tolle. In this transformative work, Tolle expands upon the concept of ego and presents a pathway towards transcending its influence, leading to a deeper state of consciousness and inner peace.

Tolle emphasizes the importance of living in the present moment and disengaging from the egoic mind. He highlights how identification with the egoic self leads to a sense of lack, conflict, and suffering in individuals' lives. Through mindful presence, individuals can dis-identify from the incessant stream of egoic thoughts and emotions. By observing the ego without judgment, individuals create a space of stillness and openness that allows them to connect with a deeper level of consciousness beyond the ego.

Tolle provides practical guidance on how to apply this awareness in everyday life to resolve conflicts, dissolve negative patterns, and embrace a state of inner peace and fulfillment. He emphasizes the importance of recognizing the ego's tricks, such as creating drama, seeking attention, or holding onto grievances, and offers tools to break free from these patterns.

The central message of "A New Earth" is that the solution to the struggle between ego and unconsciousness lies in awakening to the present moment and becoming fully conscious of the ego's mechanisms, which enables them to align with their true essence and experience a profound sense of inner transformation and spiritual growth.

Throughout the book, Tolle draws from various spiritual traditions and teachings, making his insights accessible and relevant to readers from all walks of life. "A New Earth" has had a significant impact on countless individuals worldwide, offering a practical and transformative approach to resolving the inner struggle between ego and consciousness and living a life of purpose and authenticity.

"Knowing your own darkness is the best method for dealing with the darknesses of other people."

– Carl Jung,
Swiss psychiatrist and psychoanalyst
("The Portable Jung")

When a person finds themselves caught between the realms of ego and unconsciousness, they face significant challenges that can impede their personal growth and overall well-being. This state of being, characterized by an ongoing struggle between the conscious ego and the hidden depths of the unconscious mind, can give rise to a host of problems.

One of the primary issues is a lack of self-awareness. When individuals are stuck in this inner conflict, they may become disconnected from their true selves, unaware of their thoughts, emotions, and behaviors. This lack of self-awareness prevents them from understanding the root causes of their actions and the impact they have on themselves and others.

Furthermore, unresolved unconscious patterns can persist, leading to repetitive and negative behaviors. The person may find themselves trapped in the same harmful cycles, unable to break free from these self-destructive tendencies. This perpetual struggle can lead to emotional turmoil, as the ego's desires clash with the messages emanating from the unconscious mind.

The difficulties do not end there; the conflicts between ego and unconsciousness can spill into interpersonal relationships. Unresolved emotions and projections of unconscious issues onto others can create conflicts and hinder genuine connections. The focus on external validation and the need for approval can also result in inauthenticity, preventing the person from expressing their true self and desires.

Additionally, individuals stuck in this struggle may experience a sense of emptiness and lack of fulfillment. The ego's pursuit of external achievements or possessions often fails to bring lasting happiness or contentment. As a result, personal growth and development may stagnate, as the person avoids confronting their inner challenges and integrating unconscious aspects of themselves.

This disconnect from the unconscious can also limit creativity and imagination. The ego's need for control and fear of vulnerability may stifle the creative potential that lies within. Furthermore, indecisiveness and confusion can arise as the ego's desires conflict with the intuitive insights and wisdom offered by the unconscious.

Lastly, being stuck between ego and unconsciousness may lead to a disconnection from spiritual aspects of life. The ego's dominance can prevent the person from experiencing a deeper sense of purpose, interconnectedness, and spiritual awakening.

The struggle between ego and unconsciousness can have far-reaching consequences. Recognizing and addressing this inner battle is vital for individuals seeking to embark on a journey of self-awareness, healing, and integration, ultimately leading to a more balanced, authentic, and fulfilling life.

"The quieter you become, the more you can hear."

– Ram Dass,
American spiritual teacher, "Be Here Now"

Seeking guidance is the solution to come out of the struggle between ego and unconsciousness and it involves reaching out to mentors, spiritual teachers, therapists, or other sources of wisdom to gain insights and support in understanding and navigating this inner battle.

1. **Mentors and Coaches:** Seeking guidance from mentors or coaches who have expertise in psychology, spirituality, or personal development can be beneficial. They can provide practical tools to help individuals recognize and transcend the influence of the ego while exploring the depths of their unconscious mind.
2. **Spiritual Teachers and Gurus:** For those on a spiritual journey, seeking guidance from spiritual teachers and gurus can be particularly enlightening. They can offer profound insights into the nature of ego, the path of self-realization, and the integration of unconscious aspects. These teachers often provide teachings, practices, and meditative techniques to help individuals expand their consciousness beyond egoic limitations.
3. **Therapists and Counselors:** Seeking guidance from therapists or counselors specialized in-depth psychology or psychoanalysis can assist individuals in understanding the root causes of ego-driven behaviours and unconscious patterns. Through therapy, individuals can explore unresolved issues, heal past traumas, and gain self-awareness to foster a healthier relationship with the ego and unconscious mind.

4. **Spiritual and Self-Help Books:** There are numerous books and literature available that delve into the topics of ego and unconsciousness, offering valuable insights and guidance.
5. **Meditation and Mindfulness Teachers:** Seeking guidance from meditation and mindfulness teachers can help individuals develop a regular practice to cultivate self-awareness, observe the ego's fluctuations, and explore the depths of the unconscious mind.
6. **Supportive Community:** Engaging with supportive communities, such as spiritual groups or psychotherapy groups, can offer a sense of belonging and provide a safe environment to share experiences, challenges, and growth on the journey of integrating ego and unconsciousness.
7. **Self-Reflection and Inner Exploration:** While seeking external guidance is essential, individuals can also engage in self-reflection and inner exploration. Through journaling, meditation, or introspection, individuals can inquire into their egoic patterns and unconscious beliefs to gain clarity and insights.

Seeking guidance in the struggle between ego and unconsciousness involves connecting with sources of wisdom and support to navigate this inner battle effectively. By seeking external guidance and engaging in self-reflection, individuals can gain valuable insights, find healing, and foster a more harmonious relationship between the ego and unconscious mind, ultimately leading to personal growth and spiritual transformation.

> ***"Your vision will become clear only when you can lookinto your own heart. Who looks outside, dreams; who looks inside, awakes."***
>
> ***– Carl Jung,***
> ***Swiss psychiatrist and psychoanalyst***

8

NAVIGATING CHANGE AND UNCERTAINTY: ADAPTING TO LIFE'S CURVEBALLS

Change, that inexorable force shaping the very essence of existence, weaves its intricate threads through the tapestry of life, touching every facet of our journey. From the rhythmic dance of seasons to the tides of fortune that ebb and flow, change is an unwavering companion, a constant reminder of life's impermanence. Paradoxically, while change is as natural as the breath we draw, it often ushers in a sense of unease and discomfort, triggering a myriad of emotions that cascade through our being like ripples on a tranquil pond disturbed by a stone's throw.

Why does change evoke such complexity in our hearts and minds? The answer lies in the delicate balance between familiarity and the unknown. As creatures of habit, we find solace in routines and patterns that offer a sense of stability and predictability. Change, however, disrupts these well-trodden paths, challenging our sense of order and thrusting us into the uncharted territories of uncertainty. The mere prospect of relinquishing the familiar and embracing the novel can evoke emotions ranging from apprehension to anxiety.

Consider the palpable unease that accompanies a change in our daily routines, such as starting a new job or relocating to a different place. The prospect of entering unfamiliar spaces, interacting with new faces, and adjusting to novel circumstances stirs feelings of discomfort. Our minds, wired to seek the known, grapple with the unfamiliar, often amplifying the emotional weight of change.

Change also beckons us to confront the limits of our control. In a world that seems ever-changing, we strive to wield some semblance of control over our circumstances, seeking stability in an otherwise dynamic environment. Change, however, reminds us that our grasp on life's reins is tenuous, prompting a clash between our desire for control and the reality of the unforeseen. This tension can give rise to feelings of helplessness and vulnerability, further intensifying the unease that change can elicit.

The discomfort brought by change, however, is not inherently negative. Just as discomfort is a signal that our bodies need rest or nourishment, the unease prompted by change is an indicator of growth potential. It signifies that we are standing at the threshold of evolution, poised to transcend our current state and embrace new horizons. Change challenges us to adapt, to shed old skin and forge a renewed sense of self in response to the shifting landscape. In the realm of personal growth and development, it is often the discomfort of change that propels us forward. As we venture beyond our comfort zones, we test our limits, uncover hidden reservoirs of strength, and cultivate resilience. The unease of change becomes a crucible in which our character is tempered, enabling us to navigate life's challenges with greater equanimity.

Through introspection, self-awareness, and a willingness to embrace the discomfort, we can transform the discomfort and unease that change brings into catalysts for growth. The unease can morph into anticipation, and the discomfort can give way to a sense of adventure. By acknowledging the emotional spectrum that change encompasses, we can embark on a journey of transformation, recognizing that the unease is not a barrier, but a bridge to a more enriched and evolved version of ourselves.

In the book "Who Moved My Cheese?" by Dr Spencer Johnson, the author masterfully weaves a simple yet profound allegory that serves as a powerful reflection of the human experience with change and uncertainty. At its core, this allegory underscores a fundamental truth: change is a constant and inevitable aspect of existence. Johnson's narrative is centered on a universally relatable concept—cheese—which represents comfort, success, stability, and fulfillment that we seek in various aspects of our lives.

In this allegory, Johnson introduces four distinct characters—Sniff, Scurry, Hem, and Haw—each embodying different approaches to change. The maze they navigate, a metaphor for the journey of life itself, is a terrain filled with opportunities for change and new discoveries. The essence of the story lies in the characters' reactions to the shifting circumstances, primarily through their responses to the relocation of their cherished cheese.

Sniff and Scurry, portrayed as simple mice, showcase an instinctive and pragmatic approach to change. Their unwavering ability to adapt and move forward, even when faced with unexpected shifts, mirrors the qualities of resilience and adaptability. They do not overanalyze or become attached to the past; they merely embrace the present and take proactive steps to seek out new cheese. These characters represent the essence of embracing change as a natural part of life and responding to it with an open heart and mind.

On the other hand, Hem and Haw, the humanlike characters, grapple with change in a more intricate manner. Hem initially refuses to acknowledge the reality of the moving cheese, clinging to a sense of entitlement and comfort. His resistance symbolizes the inclination many of us have to deny or resist change because of fear or an attachment to the status quo. Haw, however, undergoes a transformation as he embarks on a journey of exploration, eventually realizing that change offers opportunities for growth and personal development. His progression from denial to adaptation serves as a testament to the human capacity for change and learning.

This narrative mirrors the common human responses to change that Johnson captures in the allegory. The fear of the unknown, the comfort of familiarity, and the reluctance to step into uncharted territories are emotions that resonate deeply with readers. The characters' journeys reflect our own tendencies and shed light on the transformative power of embracing change.

Then how to deal with the uneasiness brought by change? The answer is the power of adaptability.

Amidst the ever-shifting currents of life, there exists a potent antidote to the unease and discomfort brought about by change—adaptability. Like a chameleon that seamlessly changes its colors to blend with its surroundings, the power of adaptability empowers us to navigate the tempestuous waters of change with grace and resilience. It is the art of not just surviving in the face of change, but thriving amidst its challenges.

Adaptability is the faculty that allows us to flex and mold ourselves according to the demands of changing circumstances. It is the recognition that rigidity breeds resistance, whereas fluidity breeds growth. Just as a tree sways with the wind instead of standing rigidly against it, adaptability encourages us to embrace the currents of change rather than fight against them.

One of the profound insights that the book imparts is the stark contrast between Sniff and Scurry's swift adaptation and Hem and Haw's initial resistance to change. The former, much like seasoned adapters, instinctively sense the shifting tides and promptly set out in pursuit of new cheese. Their adaptability enables them to transition smoothly from one state to another, irrespective of the challenges they encounter.

In the realms of personal and professional growth, adaptability emerges as a paramount virtue. As we embark on journeys of self-improvement, career advancement, or relationship development, we inevitably encounter changes that test our mettle. The ability to adapt becomes our secret weapon—a tool that empowers us to turn setbacks into stepping stones and challenges into opportunities.

Consider the landscape of the business world, where technological advancements and market fluctuations are constants. Companies that thrive are those that embrace adaptability as a core tenet. They pivot their strategies in response to changing consumer preferences, harness innovative technologies, and foster a culture that embraces change. This adaptability not only ensures their survival but propels them ahead of the curve.

On an individual level, adaptability cultivates resilience. It teaches us to detach from fixed outcomes and embrace the process of evolution. Like a skilled surfer riding the waves, an adaptable individual rides the waves of change, finding balance amidst the undulating currents. Moreover, adaptability nurtures a growth mindset—a belief that challenges are opportunities in disguise.

The power of adaptability is the elixir that transforms the discomfort of change into the alchemy of growth. It teaches us that change is not to be feared, but embraced as a teacher and catalyst. By cultivating adaptability, we liberate ourselves from the clutches of resistance, and instead, dance harmoniously with the rhythm of life's changes.

As we journey through the landscape of our lives, let us heed the lessons of adaptability that nature herself whispers. Let us learn to flow with the currents of change, allowing them to shape us into more resilient, resourceful, and self-aware beings. In this dance of adaptability, we not only conquer the unease of change but harness its transformative power to evolve into the best versions of ourselves.

"Progress is impossible without change, and those who cannot change their minds cannot change anything."
– George Bernard Shaw

To explain my point further, let's delve in the life of a farmer named Raj who learned and took the chance to change his mentality and prospered.

In a quaint Indian village nestled between rolling hills and fertile fields, lived a villager named Raj. Raj had spent his entire life tending to his family's small piece of farmland, cultivating crops and reaping the rewards of his labor. Life in the village was peaceful, and the routines were predictable, much like the cycle of the seasons.

One day, an unexpected guest arrived in the village. He spoke of a new irrigation system that could revolutionize farming practices, promising higher yields and more efficient water usage. While some villagers were intrigued, many, including Raj, were apprehensive about the proposed changes. They were comfortable with their traditional ways and were hesitant to embrace the unfamiliar.

As time passed, the monsoon patterns shifted, and the once-reliable rains became erratic. The crops withered, and the villagers' worries turned into reality. The old methods of farming were no longer sufficient to ensure their survival. Faced with these challenges, the villagers were forced to reconsider their resistance to change.

Raj, recognizing the dire situation, decided to listen to the newcomer's ideas. He saw the necessity of adapting to the changing climate and the potential benefits of the new irrigation system. With an open mind, he attended the workshops and learned the techniques. He was amazed at how the new system efficiently distributed water, even during periods of scarcity.

Putting his newfound knowledge to use, Raj implemented the irrigation system on his farm. Despite the initial challenges of learning and adjusting, he persisted. To his delight, his crops flourished. The village noticed Raj's success, and slowly, others began to adopt the new methods as well.

As the years went by, the village transformed. Adaptability had not only saved their crops but had elevated their way of life. The villagers realized that change was not just a disruption; it was an opportunity for growth. With newfound resilience and openness, they faced the uncertainties of weather, market fluctuations, and technological advancements.

Raj became a respected figure in the village, not just for his bountiful harvests but for his willingness to embrace change and share his learnings. He understood that adaptability was the key to survival and progress, and he became an advocate for blending tradition with innovation.

In the end, the once-reluctant villagers learned that change was not to be feared, but embraced. With adaptability as their guiding light, they thrived amidst the shifting tides, forever grateful for the lesson that had redefined their relationship with the winds of change.

Uncertainty is divine guidance. It urges you to trust in God.

Embracing uncertainty is a profound skill that requires a unique blend of courage, open-mindedness, and a willingness to venture into the unknown. One individual who exemplified this trait through a personal experience is Steve Jobs, the co-founder of Apple Inc. His journey through uncertainty serves as a testament to the transformative power of embracing the unpredictable.

In 1985, Steve Jobs was famously ousted from Apple, the company he had co-founded and nurtured into a technological powerhouse. This turn of events was undoubtedly a blow to Jobs' ego and ambitions. However, Jobs' response to this unexpected setback demonstrated his remarkable ability to embrace uncertainty.

During his time away from Apple, Jobs founded NeXT Computer, a company that aimed to produce advanced workstations for the education and business sectors. This venture was marked by numerous challenges, including the complexities of hardware design, software development, and fierce competition in the industry. Despite the uncertainties that NeXT faced, Jobs channeled his energy into creating products that were ahead of their time.

The NeXT project was not an immediate commercial success, but Jobs' resilience and his ability to embrace the uncertain outcomes of his endeavor remained steadfast. The experience honed his skills as a leader, deepened his understanding of design and innovation, and allowed him to explore new avenues.

Years later, in 1996, uncertainty led Jobs back to Apple. The company he had co-founded was now struggling, and its future was far from certain. It was in this moment of uncertainty that Jobs stepped back into the fold, bringing with him the lessons learned from NeXT and a renewed vision for Apple's future.

Jobs' return marked the beginning of a remarkable resurgence for Apple. His innovative thinking led to the creation of groundbreaking products like the iMac, iPod, iPhone, and iPad. Apple transformed from a struggling company to a global tech giant, largely because of Jobs' ability to navigate uncertainty and to leverage it as a platform for reinvention.

The story of Steve Jobs illustrates how embracing uncertainty can lead to transformative outcomes. Jobs did not shy away from the unknown; he leaned into it, used it as a springboard for growth, and harnessed it as a catalyst for innovation. His experiences with both NeXT and his return to Apple underscore that uncertain paths can lead to unexpected opportunities, growth, and success.

In a world characterized by rapid change and ambiguity, Steve Jobs' journey serves as a beacon of inspiration. It reminds us that by embracing uncertainty, we open ourselves up to a world of possibilities.

Success isn't always a bullseye; failures teach, resilience and a positive mindset lead the way.

Achieving success is not a linear process where every attempt results in hitting the target. Instead, it acknowledges that setbacks and failures are integral components of the path to success. Failures provide us with insights into what went wrong, what needs improvement, and how we can refine our strategies for future attempts.

This also highlights the significance of resilience. Resilience refers to the ability to bounce back from adversity and setbacks. It involves maintaining a determined and persistent attitude even in the face of challenges. Failures and disappointments can be disheartening, but cultivating resilience allows us to see them as temporary setbacks and learning experiences rather than permanent defeats.

Moreover, the importance of a positive mindset is underscored. A positive mindset is a mental attitude characterized by optimism, hope, and a belief in the possibility of success. When we approach challenges with a positive outlook, we not only boost our emotional well-being but also enhance our problem-solving abilities. A positive mindset enables us to reframe failures as stepping stones towards success. It allows us to focus on the lessons learned and the progress made, rather than dwelling on the setbacks themselves.

Viewing life as a battleground illustrates the idea that success is not handed to us; it's something we must actively strive for. Just as warriors prepare for battle with strategic plans and unwavering determination, individuals pursuing success must equip themselves with the tools of resilience and a positive mindset. The battlefield is not only external but also internal—within our minds and attitudes.

"Life is either a daring adventure or nothing at all."
– Helen Keller

In my life, I have a simple strategy that I follow and I would like to share it here with you as well in the hope that this will help you in your life as well.

PRACTICAL STRATEGIES FOR NAVIGATING CHANGE AND UNCERTAINTY:

Change is often accompanied by a mix of emotions, and navigating uncertainty can be challenging. To help individuals effectively cope with and even thrive amidst change, a range of practical strategies can be employed. These strategies empower individuals to approach change with mindfulness, resilience, and a proactive mindset.

Mindfulness and Grounding Techniques: Mindfulness meditation and grounding exercises offer powerful tools to stay centered and present. Mindfulness involves focusing on the present moment without judgment. Techniques such as deep breathing, body scans, and guided meditation can help reduce anxiety and increase self-awareness. Grounding exercises, on the other hand, involve connecting with the physical environment, using techniques like the 5-4-3-2-1 exercise (noticing five things you can see, four things you can touch, three things you can hear, two things you can smell, and one thing you can taste). These practices provide a sense of calm and help individuals manage the stress associated with change.

Setting Realistic Expectations: Setting realistic expectations allows individuals to approach change with patience and understanding. Acknowledge that adjustments may be gradual and that setbacks are a natural part of the journey. By doing so, the pressure to achieve instant outcomes is alleviated, fostering a healthier mindset and reducing the potential for frustration.

Creating a Support System: Change can be emotionally taxing, and having a support system in place is crucial. Reach out to friends, family, mentors, or even professional networks that offer understanding, empathy, and guidance. Sharing experiences and learning from others who have navigated similar changes can provide reassurance that you're not alone in your journey. Personal Growth Action Steps: Taking proactive steps to engage with change and uncertainty can empower you to make the most of the situation. Consider setting achievable goals that align with your personal growth objectives. These goals could include learning new skills, seeking out opportunities for growth within the changing circumstances, or stepping out of your comfort zone.

Incorporating these strategies into your approach to change and uncertainty allows you to navigate transitions with resilience and grace. The combination of these strategies equips you with the tools needed to not only weather the storms of change but to also harness their potential for personal growth and a more enriching life experience.

"Change is the law of life. And those who look only to the past or present are certain to miss the future."

– John F Kennedy

In the grand tapestry of life, change and uncertainty are threads intricately woven into our existence. The chapters of our journey are often marked by unexpected shifts, both subtle and profound, that challenge our sense of stability and familiarity. As we traverse these winding paths, the unease and discomfort that accompany change can cast a shadow on our perceptions, obscuring the transformative potential that lies within.

Yet, in embracing change, we unearth a treasure trove of opportunities for growth, resilience, and personal evolution. Through the lens of mindfulness and the practice of grounding techniques, we learn to stand firmly in the present, enabling us to navigate the waves of change with a sense of calm and centeredness. By setting realistic expectations, we free ourselves from the burden of instant gratification, allowing change to unfold naturally and granting ourselves the grace to adapt over time.

The tapestry of change becomes even richer as we weave our stories together, creating a support system that shelters us from the storm of uncertainty. This network of connections provides solace and strength, reminding us that we are never truly alone in our journey. Within the embrace of this community, we find the courage to embrace our vulnerabilities and seek guidance, discovering that shared experiences are powerful sources of wisdom.

Ultimately, change becomes not just a challenge to overcome, but a canvas upon which we paint our personal growth. By engaging in actionable steps that fuel our development, we rise above the unease, harnessing the energy of change to fuel our aspirations. Just as the caterpillar embraces its cocoon to emerge as a butterfly, we too can transform our discomfort into the wings of transformation.

9

GRATITUDE AND RESILIENCE: CULTIVATING A POSITIVE MINDSET

"Let us rise up and be thankful, for if we didn't learn a lot today, at least we learned a little, and if we didn't learn a little, at least we didn't get sick, and if we got sick, at least we didn't die; so, let us all be thankful."

– Buddha

Being thankful and having a resilient spirit are two threads that, when woven together, can create an interesting story of one's capacity for growth, strength, and overall well-being. The trip we are on will inevitably bring us companions such as change, uncertainty, and obstacles, which will color the canvas of our experiences with both vivid hues and melancholy shadows. The skill of building a positive mindset, which is a mindset that accepts thankfulness for the present and nourishes resilience for the future, finds its essence within this nuanced interaction.

We are given the gift of perspective when we practice gratitude, which is typically characterized as a loving embrace of appreciation for the benefits that life has bestowed upon us. It is a reminder to enjoy the moments of delight, no matter how ephemeral they may be, and an antidote to the cacophony of discontentment that surrounds us. The attitude of thankfulness encourages us to change our emphasis from what we do not have to what we do have, which helps to cultivate feelings of contentment and a sense of connectedness to the world in which we live.

On the other hand, resilience emerges as the armor of the soul, a quality that prepares us to navigate the storms that life may unroll for us. It is the capacity to flex without breaking, to get back up after getting knocked down, and to find fortitude under trying circumstances. The development of resilience does not guarantee a life free of difficulties; rather, it equips us to face adversity with a dogged determination and an unshakable faith in our ability to survive and thrive in spite of adversity.

The combination of being grateful with having a resilient mindset creates a symbiotic relationship that strengthens the impact of being positive. Being grateful makes us more resilient because it makes us aware that there is always something to be thanks for, regardless of the circumstances we find ourselves in. In exchange, resilience enables us to confront adversity with an attitude of thankfulness, recognizing that each test is an opportunity for personal development and advancement.

THE MAGIC CALLED GRATITUDE EXPLAINED BY PAULO COELHO

In the entrancing pages of Paulo Coelho's masterwork, "The Alchemist," we meet Santiago, a shepherd kid who is setting out on a journey to unearth his personal legend, or his genuine reason for existing in this world. Santiago's journey is a metaphor for the transformational power of gratitude, a force that changes the ordinary into the extraordinary and directs him toward his destiny. The voyage takes place amidst vast deserts and otherworldly vistas, and serves as a metaphor for the power of transformation.

The journey that Santiago must take is not without of difficulties and unpredictability. In the middle of the desert, he comes across a crystal dealer whose shop has been failing for many years. The merchant has had the ambition to go on a pilgrimage to Mecca for a very long time, but he cannot move past his anxiety and the monotony of his daily life. He cannot abandon the things that are known to him in order to pursue his desire.

As Santiago continues to work for the merchant, he makes a little adjustment, which entails reorganizing the way crystals are displayed in the shop. The energy of the area is shifted by this uncomplicated action, which encourages the presence of curious clients and invigorates the business of the vendor. The attitude of thankfulness for the chance to contribute permeates Santiago's outlook, and his upbeat energy is felt by all those who come into contact with him.

This scene shows the power of thankfulness, which is the ability to imbue the ordinary with a sense of meaning and to elevate the ordinary into the remarkable. Because Santiago is so appreciative that he was given the opportunity to assist, his position shifts from that of a simple laborer to that of an agent of transformation.

The next step in Santiago's adventure is when he meets the Alchemist, a knowledgeable sage who shares profound insights with him. Coelho emphasizes the idea that the cosmos conspires in favour of those who approach life with a heart that is full of gratitude through the various encounters that Santiago has throughout the book. Santiago can realign himself with the currents of change and open the doors to his true destiny as he gains an appreciation for the lessons that thankfulness teaches him to embrace.

The lesson that the book imparts to us is that gratitude is more than just a transient feeling; rather, it is a guiding principle that has the potential to change our path. In the same way that Santiago's thankfulness brought new life into the crystal merchant's business, our own gratitude has the power to bring new life into every facet of our existence, from the people we interact with and the things we try to do in our careers to the changes that occur within ourselves.

We would be well to pay attention to Santiago's trip and the lessons it teaches us as we make our way through the maze that is our lives. Similar to Santiago's travels, the practice of gratitude possesses the ability to transform the ordinary into the remarkable, to lead us through times of uncertainty, and to clear the path for us to find our own Personal Legends. When we cultivate thankfulness, we align ourselves with the beneficent currents of the universe, and when we do this, we unearth the magic that lies within the simple act of appreciating the beauty and benefits that surround us. Thankfulness helps us align ourselves with the benign currents of the cosmos.

THE INFLUENCE OF GRATITUDE ON ONE'S MENTAL AND EMOTIONAL WELL-BEING

Researchers in the scientific community have investigated the effects that gratitude has on the brain, and their findings have uncovered a wide range of advantages that are felt throughout our cognitive and emotional spheres.

The neurological alterations that are generated by gratitude practices have been partially revealed by research conducted with neuroimaging techniques such as functional magnetic resonance imaging (fMRI). According to the findings of these studies, the practice of expressing gratitude stimulates regions of the brain that are connected with pleasure, reward, and social bonding. When people express gratitude toward others, they stimulate the reward center of their brains, specifically the ventral striatum. This contributes to the development of a sense of well-being and positive reinforcement. Furthermore, the anterior cingulate cortex, which is responsible for processing social relationships and empathy, is engaged during expressions of appreciation, enhancing interpersonal connections and emotional resonance.

'Gratitude acts as a buffer against negative emotions and promotes emotional regulation and resilience.'

Studies have shown that persons who frequently practice gratitude demonstrate improved emotional regulation, which enables them to negotiate hard situations with serenity. This is because they are aware of the benefits that they receive from practicing thankfulness. The sensations of tension, worry, and despair can all be alleviated by cultivating an attitude of gratitude.

Gratitude acts as a buffer against unpleasant emotions. Emotional resilience can be developed by individuals by cultivating the ability to shift their focus from sources of stress to sources of thankfulness and enables them to meet change and uncertainty with a more controlled demeanor.

Gratitude works best when it is reciprocated. When we show thankfulness to others, not only do we have a positive emotional response but also the people who are on the receiving end of our gratitude gain from it. These acts of generosity promote a reciprocal loop of gratitude and positivity, so establishing a virtuous circle of well-being within social networks.

Gratitude has a reach that extends beyond its immediate emotional impact, and it can even improve overall life happiness. Multiple cross-sectional and longitudinal studies have found a correlation between an enhanced sense of thankfulness and an increased level of happiness and contentment with one's life. People who make it a habit to express thankfulness are more likely to feel that their lives have meaning and fulfillment because they cultivate an attitude that allows them to acknowledge and appreciate even life's smallest pleasures and gifts. The influence that thankfulness has on a person's mental and emotional health is a topic that is garnering an increasing amount of attention and validation in the domain of scientific research. The neurobiological shifts, emotional regulation, social connections, and increased life satisfaction that result from an attitude of thankfulness serve as foundational components for the development of a more positive mentality. As we traverse the maze of change, this knowledge allows us to harness the benefits of gratitude.

> ***"Gratitude can transform common days into thanksgivings, turn routine jobs into joy, and change ordinary opportunities into blessings."***
>
> ***– William Arthur Ward***

The fabric of our lives is woven together by the consistent behaviors that we perform daily; these rituals are the threads. The act of practicing thankfulness is one of these rituals that stands out as a powerful thread that has the potential to infuse our days with optimism, mindfulness, and a greater connection to the here and now. It is not merely a duty to make thankfulness a daily habit; rather, it is a deliberate choice that enables us to colour our lives with the shades of appreciation and contentment. Recognizing the gifts that are all around us reawakens a sense of appreciation that colours our perspective of the activities of the day, and this can happen in a variety of ways, including writing in a notebook, engaging in silent contemplation, or making verbal affirmations.

Dedicate a few minutes of each day to writing down things for which you are thankful, in a thankfulness diary. This could be anything from a thoughtful act from a friend to a breathtaking sunset or even just a brief moment of laughter. As you turn the pages, you will discover a rich tapestry of optimism that will serve as a gentle reminder of the abundance that exists in your life.

In the midst of the chaos of our daily routines, adopting thoughtful moments into our lives enables us to pause and appreciate the blessings that life has to offer. Find a routine that you can do every day to fully engage all of your senses. Note the flavor of the food you consume, the feeling your feet get when they touch the ground, and the stunning masterpieces that nature has made. This practice of mindfulness deepens your connection to the here and now, which helps you to cultivate an attitude of gratitude.

The benefits that we derive from the act of practicing appreciation are amplified when we share those benefits with others. Make it a habit to show appreciation to the people in your life, whether through a warm and honest thank-you note, a sincere praise, or a straightforward "I appreciate you." You can contribute to a good ripple effect that will improve both the collective energy surrounding you and your connections with others if you extend your expressions of thankfulness beyond just yourself.

Take some time to think about everything that happened over the day before you go to sleep. Think about the experiences that made you laugh and smile, the obstacles that pushed you to become a better person, and the relationships that added value to your life. Acknowledge these events with gratitude and allow them to act as guiding lights for you as you relax and take some time off.

The expression of appreciation through the practice of daily rituals does not require a monumental act; rather, it consists of a series of minor decisions that, when taken together, create a rich tapestry of the positive. You can transform your viewpoint from the search of more to the embrace of what currently exists in the world by including moments of appreciation into your daily activities.

> ***"Gratitude makes sense of our past, brings peace for today, and creates a vision for tomorrow."***
>
> ***– Melody Beattie***

In the annals of history, the lives of extraordinary people frequently shed light on the transformational potential of gratitude as a directing force. Think about the life of Oprah Winfrey, who is a media magnate, philanthropist, and advocate for constructive social change who is known all over the world. Oprah's daily practice of thankfulness shines as a monument to the impact that it has had on defining both her mindset and her accomplishments.

The path to popularity and power that Oprah has followed has been littered with both victories and setbacks. Her journey from a difficult childhood to becoming one of the most prominent figures in the world exemplifies a spirit of resilience and drive, and it is a testament to her character.

Oprah has made keeping a gratitude diary a lifelong discipline, and she frequently discusses it in interviews and her own writings. This is a routine that she has kept up for many years. She makes it a point to sit down at the end of each day and write down five things for which she is thankful. These entries cover a wide variety of topics, ranging from the significant impact that her philanthropic work had to the straightforward pleasures that may be found in everyday life, such as the coziness of a cup of tea or an honest talk with a close friend.

Oprah's practice of writing in a thankfulness diary daily has not only helped her remain stable during times of transition and unpredictability, but it has also served as a source of the upbeat attitude that permeates everything she does and does.

The significant effect that cultivating an attitude of appreciation can have on one's life is highlighted by Oprah's example. She has developed a mindset that exudes positivity and resiliency because of consciously cultivating a practice that recognizes and appreciates the gifts that life has bestowed upon her. As we gain insight from Oprah's journey, we come to the realization that thankfulness is not limited to abstract concepts; rather, it is a functional instrument that enables us to exert agency over our lives and the world around us. The practice of gratitude can illuminate our pathways, nurture our spirits, and guide us toward a future marked by resiliency, purpose, and a profound feeling of fulfillment.

> ***"In the end, though, maybe we must all give up trying to pay back the people in this world who sustain our lives.***
> ***In the end, maybe it's wiser to surrender before the miraculous scope of human generosity and to just keep saying thank you, forever and sincerely, for as long as we have voices."***

– Elizabeth Gilbert

10

THE PARADOX OF CHOICE: SIMPLIFYING DECISIONS IN A WORLD OF ENDLESS OPTIONS

In a world marked by remarkable progress and unparalleled access to information, we find ourselves standing at the crossroads of abundance and complexity. From selecting our morning coffee to making life-altering decisions, our daily lives are peppered with choices. In theory, the freedom to choose should empower us, allowing us to craft lives uniquely tailored to our desires and aspirations. However, a closer examination reveals a fascinating paradox that lies beneath the surface—the paradox of choice.

Imagine strolling down the aisle of a supermarket, your eyes scanning the shelves filled with seemingly infinite brands and flavors of cereal. The coffee shop menu presents you with a bewildering assortment of latte combinations, each more elaborate than the last. As you navigate your career, you're confronted with an abundance of paths to take, each holding its own allure and potential—characterized by choice on a scale never before witnessed in human history.

In this pursuit of abundance, what appears to be a boon, an ever-expanding menu of choices, has given rise to the paradox of choice, a phenomenon that disrupts the harmony between our desires and our ability to make decisions.

This paradox isn't limited to supermarket shelves and cafe menus; it extends across every facet of our existence. From the small decisions that frame our daily routines to the monumental choices that shape the trajectory of our lives, the constant influx of options has profound implications for our well-being, happiness, and personal growth.

As we embark on a journey to explore the intricacies of the paradox of choice, we'll delve into the cognitive processes that influence how we make decisions, examining why an abundance of choices doesn't always lead to the satisfaction and fulfillment we anticipate. Together, we'll uncover the hidden costs of choice overload—the stress, anxiety, and dissatisfaction that can result from navigating an ocean of possibilities.

But this exploration isn't meant to instill a sense of resignation or despair. Instead, our aim is to equip you with the knowledge and strategies to navigate the labyrinth of choices more effectively. We'll examine the art of simplifying decisions, of striking a balance between the quest for variety and the need for clarity. By understanding the mechanisms at play, we can liberate ourselves from decision paralysis and the nagging "what-ifs" that accompany every choice.

THE BIGGEST DEMON - 'WHAT IF'

'What ifs' can become problematic because of their psychological and emotional impact on decision-making and overall well-being. Continuously pondering potential alternative outcomes and choices can lead to decision paralysis, making it difficult to make choices because of fear of regret. Additionally, the idealized nature of 'what ifs' can create unrealistic expectations that real-world choices can't fulfill, resulting in ongoing dissatisfaction. Even after decisions are made, lingering 'what ifs' can diminish the ability to fully appreciate chosen paths and reduce overall life satisfaction. This stress can negatively affect mental and physical well-being. Furthermore, 'what ifs' can lead to feelings of retroactive regret, causing individuals to look back on past choices with remorse. This type of regret is counterproductive, as it prevents individuals from fully engaging in their present circumstances and experiences.

The mental energy invested in 'what ifs' can distract from the present moment, hinder personal growth, and undermine learning opportunities. It can also strain relationships by introducing doubt and insecurity, eroding trust and creating misunderstandings. The constant questioning of choices due to 'what ifs' can damage self-confidence and belief in one's decision-making abilities. Lastly, overthinking 'what ifs' consumes mental and emotional energy that could be directed towards more productive endeavors, leading to burnout and reduced effectiveness.

HOW TO DEAL WITH 'WHAT-IFS'?

The nagging "what ifs" that accompany our choices can feel like persistent echoes in our minds, reverberating long after a decision has been made. These hypothetical scenarios, often tinged with doubt and regret, are central to the experience of the paradox of choice. Fortunately, psychology offers valuable insights on how to navigate and alleviate the grip of these 'what ifs':

Mindfulness and Present-Centeredness: Psychologists often advocate for mindfulness—the practice of being fully present in the moment. By focusing our attention on the present, we ground ourselves in reality and reduce the propensity for rumination.

Cognitive Restructuring: Cognitive behavioral therapy (CBT) teaches us to challenge and reframe negative thought patterns. When confronted with 'what ifs', psychologists encourage us to evaluate the evidence for these scenarios. Are they based on factual information or emotional assumptions? By examining the basis of our worries, we can counterbalance the pull of hypothetical regrets.

Positive Visualization: Cognitive techniques often include positive visualization. Instead of fixating on negative 'what ifs', psychologists suggest envisioning positive outcomes and focusing on potential benefits. By actively visualizing success and satisfaction, we can reshape our thought patterns and mitigate the sense of missed opportunities.

Acceptance and Commitment: The psychological approach of acceptance and commitment therapy (ACT) emphasizes embracing our emotions rather than trying to suppress them. When grappling with 'what ifs', we can acknowledge our fears and doubts without getting entangled in them. This acceptance creates psychological space for making decisions based on our values and aspirations.

Learning from Experience: Rather than viewing 'what ifs' as sources of distress, they can serve as valuable learning opportunities. Reflecting on our decisions, even the ones that lead to less favorable outcomes, can provide insights for future choices and personal growth.

Setting Realistic Expectations: Psychologists encourage us to set realistic expectations for ourselves and our decisions. Acknowledging that there's rarely a single "best" choice can help us approach our decisions with greater self-compassion and a reduced burden of unrealistic regret.

Constructive Self-Talk: Psychologists promote constructive self-talk as a way to counteract the negative impact of 'what ifs'. Instead of engaging in self-criticism, we can consciously direct our inner dialogue toward self-encouragement and affirmation.

Implementing Decision Deadlines: The 'what ifs' can thrive in the space of indecision. Psychologists suggest setting decision deadlines to prevent overthinking. This time-bound approach forces us to evaluate our options, make a choice, and then shift our focus toward making the chosen path successful rather than dwelling on alternatives.

Incorporating these psychological strategies into your decision-making process can help you confront 'what ifs' with resilience and clarity. Remember that while it's human nature to wonder about the paths not taken, your focus on embracing the power of choice and cultivating present-centered awareness will guide you towards a more fulfilling and growth-oriented perspective.

> ***"When you own your choices, you hold the pen that writes the script of your life's journey."***

In his book "The Paradox of Choice: Why More Is Less", psychologist Barry Schwartz sheds light on how the abundance of choices in modern society can lead to anxiety, dissatisfaction, and a sense of overwhelm.

Schwartz argues that while having options is certainly desirable, an excess of choices can actually hinder our ability to make decisions and find contentment. He presents the notion that beyond a certain point, the ever-expanding array of choices tends to overload our cognitive processes. This leads to a phenomenon he coins as "choice paralysis," where individuals find themselves unable to decide because of the fear of making the wrong one.

One of the key concepts Schwartz introduces is the "maximizer" vs "satisficer" distinction. Maximizers are those who seek to make the absolute best choice in every situation. They exhaustively research and compare all available options, often feeling overwhelmed by the volume of information. Satisficers, on the other hand, are content with a choice that meets their criteria, even if it might not be the absolute best option. Schwartz suggests that satisficers tend to experience greater well-being and satisfaction because they don't get caught in the endless cycle of second-guessing.

Schwartz also delves into the psychological toll of constantly contemplating the "what ifs". He points out that the sheer number of potential paths and outcomes can lead to a nagging sense of regret—the feeling that any decision could have been better. This emotional burden can erode our ability to fully enjoy the choices we do make, trapping us in a cycle of perpetual dissatisfaction.

To address these challenges, Schwartz suggests practical strategies. One is the idea of "good enough" decision-making. This involves setting clear criteria for choices, making a decision once those criteria are met, and then moving forward without looking back. Another strategy is to focus on experiences rather than possessions. By shifting our attention from material accumulation to meaningful experiences, we can reduce the pressure of constantly needing to make the "perfect" choice.

Schwartz's book serves as a comprehensive exploration of the paradox of choice and its far-reaching implications. Through his research, Schwartz not only validates the reality of the paradox but also offers a roadmap for finding greater contentment and fulfillment amidst the sea of choices we encounter every day.

LEARNING THE ART OF 'LETTING GO'

In the intricate tapestry of life, we often find ourselves entangled in the threads of attachments, expectations, and memories. The concept of letting go emerges as a profound and transformative practice, offering a way to navigate the complexities of existence with greater clarity and freedom. It's an art that, when mastered, can liberate us from the burdens of the past, the uncertainties of the future, and the constraints of our own emotions.

Letting go is not synonymous with indifference or detachment; rather, it's an invitation to release the grip of control over situations and outcomes that are beyond our influence. It's an acknowledgment that, despite our best efforts, we cannot control every facet of life. Through letting go, we create space for growth, resilience, and a deeper connection with the present moment.

At its core, letting go is an act of surrender—a surrender of our attachment to specific outcomes and our need to micromanage every aspect of our lives. It's a recognition that life is fluid, and change is inevitable. Whether it's a past mistake, an unfulfilled desire, or a lingering resentment, the art of letting go involves loosening our grip on what we cannot change.

A pivotal aspect of letting go is cultivating acceptance of the present moment as it is, without judgment or resistance. It's about embracing the imperfections, uncertainties, and even the discomfort that life can bring and open ourselves up to the beauty of each moment.

Meditation and mindfulness practices play a significant role in this process, as they train our minds to observe thoughts and emotions without getting entangled in them. Additionally, journaling, seeking support from loved ones, and engaging in creative endeavors can facilitate the journey of letting go.

In the pages that follow, we'll embark on a journey of exploration and practice, delving into the nuances of letting go. We'll uncover the psychological underpinnings of attachment, the profound impact of acceptance, and practical techniques to cultivate this art in our daily lives. As we navigate the waters of letting go, may we find ourselves lighter, more resilient, and deeply connected to the rhythm of life itself.

> ***"The more you have, the more you are occupied. The less you have, the more free you are."***
>
> ***– Mother Teresa***

EMBRACING REGRET: A SHIFT IN PERSPECTIVE

Regret is a natural and complex human emotion that often arises when we reflect on past choices and actions. It's a sentiment that can linger, gnawing at our thoughts and emotions, making us question the paths we've taken. However, within the realm of personal growth and emotional well-being, there exists a transformative perspective: understanding that if it was your own decision, there's no need for regret.

Decisions are made within the context of the information, experiences, and emotions available to us at a particular moment in time. Hindsight, while valuable for learning, doesn't always provide the same clarity that we possess now. Acknowledging this context allows us to embrace the idea that we did the best we could with what we had.

Regret often arises from recognizing the gap between our past choices and our current understanding. This realization can be a catalyst for growth, prompting us to refine our decision-making processes and align our actions with our evolving values.

Regret often stems from imagining an idealized outcome that contrasts with reality. Yet, if we fully understood the complexities of a situation when we made a choice, we might have found that the outcome we hoped for wasn't realistically attainable. By letting go of the attachment to an ideal result, we free ourselves from the chains of regret.

Embracing the understanding that we did what we believed was right at the time nurtures self-compassion. Instead of berating ourselves for not knowing better, we extend kindness to our past selves. This self-compassion lays the foundation for forgiveness, healing, and a healthier relationship with our decisions.

Regret need not be a stagnant emotion. It can be a catalyst for proactive steps toward positive change. If we identify a pattern of regrettable decisions, we can use this insight to inform future choices. Regret becomes a roadmap for aligning our actions with our aspirations.

Every decision, even those that lead to regret, contributes to our growth and evolution. It's a testament to our willingness to take risks, make choices, and learn from our experiences. By embracing our journey, including the missteps, we celebrate our resilience and capacity for change. By integrating this perspective into our mindset, we pave the way for a more empowered and enriched journey through life's choices.

> ***"Choice is a powerful tool; choose wisely, and it can lead to liberation. Choose poorly, and it can become a prison."***
>
> ***– Unknown***

In a quiet town nestled between rolling hills, lived a man named Vijay. He had spent his life as an accomplished painter, creating vibrant canvases that captured the essence of nature's beauty. As Vijay grew older, he found himself haunted by a particular regret: the unfinished painting that had sat untouched in his studio for years.

The painting was meant to be a masterpiece—a reflection of the kaleidoscope of colors he had witnessed during a particularly breathtaking sunrise. However, Vijay's initial attempts to capture its brilliance on the canvas fell short of his expectations. Frustration grew, and eventually, he stashed the incomplete work away, overwhelmed by a sense of disappointment.

As the years passed, Vijay's regret over the unfinished painting began to overshadow his joy in painting itself. He would often sit in his studio, staring at the canvas with a mix of longing and self-criticism. His friends and family urged him to finish the painting, but he resisted, convinced that completing it was an impossible task.

One day, as Vijay gazed out of his window, he noticed a vibrant rainbow stretching across the sky after a sudden rainstorm. The colors were reminiscent of the very hues that had eluded him in his unfinished painting. The sight sparked a realization: he had been burdening himself with an unattainable vision, failing to appreciate the beauty in his work as it was.

Vijay decided to revisit the canvas with a new perspective. Instead of striving for perfection, he embraced the imperfections that had caused him so much frustration. He allowed himself to paint freely, using the unfinished sunrise as a starting point but allowing his creativity to guide him.

As the strokes of color flowed onto the canvas, Vijay began to experience a sense of liberation. He realized that his regret had been rooted in his attachment to an ideal outcome—one that might never have been achievable. By releasing his grip on this ideal, he had created space for growth and renewal.

When Vijay finally put down his brush, he looked at the painting before him with a mixture of pride and contentment. The canvas was a beautiful blend of colors that captured the essence of the sunrise, imperfect and unique in its own right. It wasn't the masterpiece he had initially envisioned, but it was a masterpiece in its authenticity.

> ***"The canvas of life is painted with both triumphs and regrets, creating a masterpiece of experience."***

THE POWER OF A POSITIVE APPROACH TO DECISION-MAKING

Adopting a positive approach as we navigate life's crossroads becomes a cornerstone for traversing its complexities with grace and resilience. At the heart of this approach lies a series of practices that foster positivity in our decision-making process:

Cultivating Self-Awareness: Grounded decisions begin with self-awareness. By understanding our values, aspirations, and priorities, we lay a solid foundation for making choices that resonate with our authentic selves.

Gratitude as a Guiding Light: Approaching decisions from a place of gratitude sets a positive tone. When we acknowledge the abundance in our lives, we are better equipped to make choices that honor our blessings.

Mindful Reflection: Engaging in mindful reflection before deciding enables us to uncover biases, fears, or negative thought patterns that might cloud our judgment. This practice fosters clarity and informed decision-making.

Seeing Opportunities, Not Just Obstacles: By shifting our perspective from dwelling on potential pitfalls to recognizing the growth opportunities within decisions, we set ourselves up for a positive and proactive approach.

Positive Visualization: Envisioning the positive outcomes of our choices can boost our confidence and motivation. This visualization sets the stage for success, reinforcing our belief in the possibilities ahead.

Embracing the Unknown: Instead of fearing the uncertainty that accompanies decisions, we can choose to welcome it. Approaching choices with curiosity and openness transforms the unknown into an exciting journey of discovery.

Building Resilience: A positive mindset empowers resilience. Believing in our ability to navigate challenges bolsters our confidence and allows us to approach decisions with a sense of empowerment.

Affirming Confidence: Regularly affirming our capabilities contributes to self-confidence. This self-assuredness is a valuable asset when it comes to making decisions that align with our aspirations.

The ripple effect of this positive approach extends far beyond the moment of decision:

Enhanced Well-Being: Approaching decisions from a positive

mindset alleviates stress and anxiety, contributing to emotional well-being. This fosters a sense of inner peace and contentment.

Stronger Relationships: The positive choices we make often lead to approaching interactions with empathy and understanding nurtures connections and deepens bonds.

Personal Growth: Each choice made with a positive approach becomes a stepping stone toward personal growth. Regardless of the outcome, the journey itself becomes a source of enrichment.

Empowerment: The positive lens through which we view our decisions empowers us to take ownership of our lives. It reinforces the belief that we are the captains of our destinies.

Expanded Horizons: Choosing with positivity opens doors to new experiences. Embracing change and taking calculated risks can lead to unexpected and fulfilling adventures.

Radiating Influence: Our positive approach can inspire those around us. By witnessing our choices and attitude, friends, family, and even strangers can be motivated to approach life with greater positivity.

In the grand tapestry of life, each decision contributes a thread woven intricately into the fabric of our journey. By adopting a positive approach, we infuse vibrant colors into this tapestry, creating a masterpiece of resilience, growth, and joyful living.

> ***"The more choices we have, the more difficult it becomes to choose. Embrace simplicity to find the courage to decide."***

NAVIGATING RISK: THE WISDOM OF CALCULATED RISKS

Life's journey is peppered with opportunities that beckon us to venture beyond our comfort zones. Taking risks can be a gateway to growth, innovation, and extraordinary achievements. Yet, the art of wise decision-making lies in recognizing that while risk-taking is commendable, opting for calculated risks ensures a balance between ambition and prudence.

At its core, a calculated risk involves a meticulous assessment of the potential rewards against the potential consequences. It's a dance between seizing an opportunity and mitigating potential downsides.

Understanding probability is essential in calculated risk-taking, allowing you to assess the likelihood of various outcomes and make choices based on these probabilities. This approach strengthens your resilience by preparing you for contingencies, helping you consider potential challenges and devise backup plans. Moreover, it recognizes that setbacks are part of the journey, serving as valuable learning experiences.

The magic of calculated risks lies in their delicate balance. While fear of the unknown can paralyze progress, recklessness can lead to avoidable pitfalls. By embarking on calculated risks, you acknowledge the value of innovation while safeguarding your well-being and that of those who depend on you.

In a world that thrives on change and evolution, calculated risk-taking is a compass that steers you toward your dreams with wisdom and foresight. It's a testament to your courage to explore uncharted territories while embracing the lessons of the past. As you journey forward, let the winds of calculated risk carry you toward new horizons, armed with the insights to navigate the twists and turns that lie ahead.

OWNING YOUR CHOICES: EMBRACING RESPONSIBILITY AND LIVING FULLY

Life unfolds like a tapestry woven with the threads of decisions both big and small. Each choice we make contributes to the intricate pattern of our existence. As we navigate this tapestry, one principle stands out: take full responsibility for your decisions and embrace the joy of living life to the fullest.

Responsibility isn't a burden; it's a gift that empowers us to shape our lives with intention. When we take ownership of our choices, we hold the pen to our own story. Embracing responsibility is not about assigning blame; it's about recognizing that our decisions reflect our values, beliefs, and circumstances. Each choice is an opportunity to align our actions with our aspirations and to learn from the outcomes, regardless of whether they unfold as expected.

Taking responsibility for our decisions liberates us from the constraints of victimhood. It empowers us to approach challenges with a problem-solving mindset, fostering resilience and growth. Moreover, it deepens our connection to the present moment, as we fully engage with the consequences of our actions.

When we own our choices, we infuse intention into every facet of our lives. Instead of being swept along by the currents of circumstance, we become conscious architects of our journey. This intentionality enriches our experiences, enhancing the depth and meaning of every moment.

No decision comes without its share of challenges and uncertainties. Yet, by taking responsibility for our choices, we equip ourselves to face these challenges with courage and adaptability. We learn to dance gracefully with success and failure, knowing that each step contributes to the symphony of our lives.

Responsibility doesn't equate to seriousness; it invites us to revel in the delight of existence. As we savor the fruits of our decisions, we open ourselves to the full spectrum of human experience—from moments of triumph to instances of reflection and growth.

So, as you navigate the crossroads of life, let the banner of responsibility unfurl in your heart. Take ownership of your choices, relishing the power and freedom it brings. Whatever the outcome, know that you've ventured forth with purpose. Allow the tapestry of your life to be woven with the threads of responsibility, empowerment, and the unwavering commitment to embrace each moment with open arms.

> ***"Life's palette becomes vibrant when you take responsibility for the colors you choose to paint with."***

11

THE ART OF MINDFUL LIVING: EXPLORING THE BENEFITS OF PRESENT-MOMENT AWARENESS

MONKEY MIND; ARE YOU ALSO SUFFERING?

"Monkey mind" is a term that vividly captures the restless and erratic nature of human thought processes, drawing from the image of a monkey swinging from tree to tree in a jungle, never staying in one place for long. In a similar manner, the monkey mind flits from one thought to another, with little regard for continuity or coherence.

Characterized by a constant stream of consciousness, the monkey mind seldom rests. It generates an incessant flow of thoughts, ranging from worries and anxieties to daydreams and inner commentaries.

As a result, sustained focus becomes elusive, and the mind struggles to remain anchored to the present moment. This lack of mental stillness can lead to a range of negative effects on well-being and can contribute to heightened stress levels, as it often fixates on concerns and uncertainties. This can disrupt sleep, create a sense of restlessness, and hinder relaxation.

Furthermore, the monkey mind's propensity to replay past events or anticipate future scenarios can contribute to anxiety and rumination. The mind gets trapped in cycles of worry, repeatedly analyzing situations or interactions, without reaching any resolution.

Addressing the challenges posed by the monkey mind is a fundamental aspect of mindfulness practice. Mindfulness involves cultivating a non-judgmental awareness of one's thoughts, emotions, and sensations in the present moment. By observing thoughts without getting entangled in them, individuals can break the cycle of constant mental activity. Techniques such as breath awareness provide an anchor to the present, helping to mitigate the mind's tendency to wander.

Through mindful meditation, individuals develop a greater sense of detachment from their thoughts. Instead of struggling to control or suppress them, they learn to accept thoughts as transient mental events. This fosters a healthier relationship with the monkey mind, allowing individuals to observe its antics without becoming overwhelmed or consumed by them.

> ***"The practice of mindfulness begins in the small, remote cave of your unconscious mind and blossoms with the sunlight of your conscious life, reaching far beyond the people and places you can see."***
>
> ***– Earon Davis***

SOLVING THE MONKEY MIND THROUGH MINDFUL LIVING AND LIVING IN THE PRESENT

Dealing with the relentless chatter of the "monkey mind" is a common challenge in our fast-paced and distracted world. The constant stream of thoughts, worries, and mental noise can be overwhelming, leading to stress, anxiety, and a sense of being disconnected from the present moment. Mindful living and the practice of living in the present offer valuable solutions to tame the monkey mind and regain a sense of inner calm and focus.

Mindful living provides an effective solution to the monkey mind challenge by offering a systematic approach to managing the mind's wandering tendencies. At its core, mindful living encourages us to bring a gentle, non-judgmental awareness to our thoughts and experiences. Rather than attempting to control or suppress thoughts, we learn to observe them with a sense of detachment, creating a space between ourselves and our mental chatter.

Central to both mindful living and addressing the monkey mind is the practice of living in the present. Living in the present means consciously directing our attention to the current moment, rather than dwelling on the past or worrying about the future. It's about experiencing life as it unfolds, savoring each experience without the burden of constant mental commentary.

Mindful living encourages us to cultivate mindful awareness—an intentional and non-judgmental attention to the present. When we apply this awareness to the monkey mind's chatter, we begin to notice the patterns, triggers, and habits of our thoughts. This awareness provides a foundation for understanding our thought processes and gaining a sense of control over them.

Living in the present serves as a practical technique to manage the monkey mind. When we immerse ourselves in the present moment, engaging our senses and focusing on our current activity, we redirect the mind's attention from its restless jumping. By savoring the sensory experiences of the present—whether it's the taste of food, the warmth of sunlight, or the sound of birds—we anchor ourselves in the "now" and create a still point amidst the mental movement. The synergy between mindful living and living in the present is evident. Mindful living provides the tools and mindset to cultivate present-moment awareness, while the practice of living in the present reinforces mindful living. Both approaches invite us to embrace the here and now, encouraging us to shift from being mere spectators of our thoughts to becoming active participants in our experiences.

The combination of mindful living and the practice of living in the present offers a powerful antidote to the monkey mind's chaos. By developing a non-reactive awareness of our thoughts and consciously engaging with the present moment, we can gradually train the monkey mind to settle into a more peaceful and focused state. This transformation fosters mental clarity, emotional balance, and a deeper connection to the richness of each moment.

WHAT DOES BUDDHISM SAYS ABOUT IT?

Buddhism provides profound insights into the nature of the "monkey mind" and offers a rich array of teachings and practices that directly address the challenges posed by it. While the direct term "monkey mind" might not be present in Buddhist teachings, the concept of mental restlessness and the erratic nature of thoughts align closely with Buddhist perspectives.

Central to Buddhism is the recognition of the impermanent and unsatisfactory nature of worldly existence, often referred to as "dukkha" or suffering. The untrained mind, resembling the restless nature of the monkey mind, is seen as a source of suffering as it constantly seeks pleasure, avoids pain, and remains entangled in attachments.

The Buddhist approach to overcoming the monkey mind's challenges involves mindfulness and present-moment awareness. The practice of mindfulness, known as "sati" in Pali, involves observing the mind's activities without judgment. By cultivating non-reactive awareness to thoughts, feelings, and sensations, individuals can develop a healthier relationship with their mental processes.

Meditation is a cornerstone of Buddhist practice, and various meditation techniques directly address the monkey mind's tendencies. Mindfulness meditation, such as Vipassana, encourages practitioners to observe thoughts and sensations as they arise, fostering a deeper understanding of the mind's patterns and reducing its restlessness.

An essential aspect of Buddhist teachings is non-attachment, emphasizing the impermanent nature of all things. By cultivating non-attachment to thoughts and experiences, individuals can gradually untangle themselves from the grip of the monkey mind's constant seeking and aversion.

Moreover, Buddhism encourages self-observation and self-awareness. Practitioners engage in introspective practices to gain insight into their mental habits, desires, and aversions. This self-awareness facilitates a better understanding of the root causes of mental restlessness and how to address them.

The concept of the Middle Way is also significant. While the goal is not to eradicate thoughts altogether, Buddhism teaches finding a balanced approach. Instead of being swept away by thoughts or forcefully suppressing them, individuals learn to observe thoughts with equanimity, allowing them to arise and pass without undue attachment.

Right Mindfulness, a part of the Noble Eightfold Path, is a crucial principle in Buddhism. It involves being aware of one's body, feelings, mind, and phenomena in the present moment. By developing this aspect of Right Mindfulness, practitioners gain a comprehensive understanding of their mental processes and learn to navigate the monkey mind's challenges more skillfully.

Buddhism offers a comprehensive toolkit for addressing the monkey mind's restlessness. Its teachings on mindfulness, meditation, non-attachment, and self-awareness provide profound guidance on how to transform mental turbulence into clarity, equanimity, and a deeper connection with the present moment.

> ***"The art of mindful living means you are not pursuing happiness; you are enjoying the present moment."***
>
> ***– Thích Nhất Hạnh***

One famous book that extensively explores the concept of the monkey mind and its relation to mindfulness is "The Miracle of Mindfulness" by Thich Nhat Hanh. This influential book presents the teachings of Thich Nhat Hanh, a renowned Vietnamese Zen master, on the practice of mindfulness in daily life.

The book demonstrates how the practice of mindfulness offers a way to calm the monkey mind and cultivate a state of deep presence. Thich Nhat Hanh introduces various mindfulness techniques, such as conscious breathing, walking meditation, and eating meditation, which anchor our attention in the present moment. By engaging in these practices, we learn to break free from the constant cycle of thoughts and immerse ourselves fully in what we are doing.

Thich Nhat Hanh's teachings highlight the interplay between mindful living and living in the present. He encourages us to bring mindfulness to our daily activities, whether it's washing dishes, drinking tea, or walking. By doing so, we shift our focus from dwelling on the past or worrying about the future to embracing the richness of the current moment.

Furthermore, the book emphasizes the importance of non-judgmental awareness. Thich Nhat Hanh teaches that by observing our thoughts without judgment, we can create a space of understanding and compassion for ourselves. This aligns with the concept of mindful living, where we cultivate a gentle awareness of our thoughts, feelings, and experiences without the need to label them.

"The Miracle of Mindfulness" also emphasizes the significance of breathing as an anchor to the present. Thich Nhat Hanh encourages us to pay attention to our breath as a way to center ourselves and transcend the monkey mind's restlessness. By focusing on the breath, we establish a direct connection to the present moment, fostering a state of calm and clarity.

MINDFULNESS PARADOX

The concept of the "mindfulness paradox" encapsulates the intriguing duality that exists within the practice of mindfulness. On one hand, mindfulness invites us to cultivate a focused and attentive awareness of the present moment, while on the other hand, it acknowledges and accepts the ever-present nature of the wandering mind. This paradox lies at the heart of mindfulness practice and offers profound insights into the nature of human consciousness.

At its core, the mindfulness paradox recognizes that the human mind is naturally inclined to wander. Our thoughts often flit from one topic to another, carrying us away from the present into memories of the past or projections into the future.

In the mindfulness paradox, the paradoxical nature arises when we consider that mindfulness, a practice rooted in focused attention on the present, invites us to observe our wandering thoughts without judgment. It encourages us to adopt an attitude of non-reactive awareness toward our mental activity, whether it's focused or scattered.

This paradox is rich with implications:

Acceptance of Reality: Instead of striving for a perpetually focused mind, mindfulness acknowledges that the mind will wander naturally. This recognition reduces the frustration that can arise from trying to forcefully eliminate all distractions.

Non-Judgmental Observation: Mindfulness teaches us to observe our thoughts without attaching labels such as "good" or "bad" to them, which allows us to witness the wandering mind with curiosity and compassion, fostering a healthier relationship with our thoughts.

Choice in Response: By acknowledging the paradox, we gain the power to choose our response to our mental activity. We can gently guide our attention back to the present without berating ourselves for wandering thoughts, fostering a sense of self-empowerment.

Understanding Impermanence: The mindfulness paradox highlights the impermanent nature of thoughts. Just as moments arise and pass, thoughts come and go. This understanding fosters a deeper sense of impermanence and detachment from the ebb and flow of mental activity.

Embracing the Paradox: The mindfulness paradox teaches us to embrace the coexistence of focused attention and wandering thoughts.

The mindfulness paradox is a reminder that by holding both focused attention and mental wanderings in a balanced awareness, we can find harmony within the dynamic interplay of our conscious experience.

> ***"Mindfulness is the aware, balanced acceptance of the present experience. It isn't more complicated than that. It is opening to or receiving the present moment, pleasant or unpleasant, just as it is, without either clinging to it or rejecting it."***
>
> ***– Sylvia Boorstein***

WHAT DOES SCIENCE HAVE TO SAY ABOUT THIS?

From a scientific standpoint, the "monkey mind" concept aligns with certain cognitive tendencies that researchers have explored. Although the specific term might not be used, cognitive psychology acknowledges the mind's tendency to wander, often shifting between thoughts, distractions, and spontaneous mental processes. This wandering nature has been associated with the Default Mode Network (DMN), a brain network linked to mind-wandering, self-referential thinking, and daydreaming. Neuroimaging studies using techniques like MRI have revealed that the DMN tends to activate when the mind is not engaged in focused tasks, reflecting the characteristics of the monkey mind.

Mindfulness, on the other hand, has garnered extensive scientific attention for its effects on the brain and cognitive processes. Research has demonstrated that regular mindfulness meditation has been associated with increased neural plasticity, potentially contributing to better attentional control and reduced mind-wandering.

One intriguing finding is that mindfulness practice appears to modulate the activity of the DMN. Studies have indicated that mindfulness meditation can lead to decreased activation of the DMN, suggesting that the practice helps to quiet the restless mental chatter associated with the monkey mind. This reduction in DMN activity aligns with the concept of living in the present, as mindfulness encourages individuals to redirect their attention away from rumination and self-referential thinking.

Furthermore, mindfulness practice seems to enhance the activation of the prefrontal cortex—a region associated with executive functions and attentional control. This heightened activation supports the ability to regulate attention and steer it away from distractions, aligning with the practice of present-moment awareness and managing the wandering tendencies of the mind.

Mindfulness-based interventions have also shown benefits beyond neural changes. Studies indicate that mindfulness practice is linked to reduced rumination, improved attention regulation, enhanced emotional regulation, and decreased stress. These findings underscore the practical implications of mindfulness in addressing the challenges posed by the monkey mind.

YOGA CAN BE THE ANSWER

Practicing yoga can be very helpful in addressing the challenges posed by the "monkey mind" and fostering a state of mindful living. Yoga is a holistic practice that combines physical postures, breath control, meditation, and mindfulness to promote overall well-being, balance, and mental clarity.

Yoga emphasizes the connection between the body and mind. Through the practice of various asanas (physical postures), individuals engage their bodies in a mindful and focused manner. This integration of movement, breath, and awareness can help shift the mind's attention away from wandering thoughts and anchor it in the present moment.

It places great importance on breath control, known as pranayama. By synchronizing breath with movement or focusing on specific breathing patterns, individuals cultivate a heightened awareness of their breath and bodily sensations. This mindfulness of breath serves as an anchor to the present, helping to quiet the fluctuations of the mind.

Many yoga practises incorporate meditation techniques, which align with the practice of mindfulness. Savasana (corpse pose) at the end of a yoga session, for instance, provides an opportunity for deep relaxation and meditation. This practice of stillness can help calm the monkey mind and promote a sense of tranquility.

As stress and anxiety are often contributors to the restless mind, yoga's emphasis on relaxation, deep breathing, and gentle movement can alleviate these factors and create an environment conducive to present-moment awareness.

Yoga encourages individuals to tune into their bodies' sensations and messages. This heightened awareness of the body's signals can extend to an increased awareness of thoughts and emotions, enabling individuals to recognize the monkey mind's patterns and respond with mindfulness.

Yoga teaches patience and non-judgmental self-observation. As individuals encounter physical challenges or mental distractions during practice, they learn to approach these experiences with patience and self-compassion—skills that directly relate to taming the monkey mind's restlessness.

By engaging the body and mind in harmony, yoga offers a powerful tool to counteract mental restlessness and cultivate a deeper connection with the present moment.

LIVING IN PRESENT IS IMPORTANT

One of the most famous and influential personalities who extensively discussed the concept of living in the present moment was Eckhart Tolle.

In "The Power of Now," Eckhart Tolle emphasizes the importance of being fully present and aware in the current moment. He articulates how many of our mental and emotional challenges arise from dwelling on the past or worrying about the future, which prevents us from truly experiencing the richness of the present.

Tolle introduces the idea of the "pain-body," a term he uses to describe accumulated emotional pain and suffering that arises from living in a state of past regrets or future anxieties. He suggests that by practicing presence and mindfulness, individuals can gradually dissolve the pain-body and experience greater peace and contentment.

Throughout the book, Tolle provides practical guidance on how to cultivate mindfulness and embrace the present moment. He shares insights on how to break free from the constant stream of thoughts and ego-driven mental patterns that hinder our ability to live in the now.

> ***"The insatiable curiosity about the future can erode the beauty of the present moment."***

The allure of the future and the temptation to constantly

anticipate what lies ahead can be a powerful force that pulls us away from the present moment. This phenomenon, often associated with the concept of the monkey mind, reflects our innate human tendency to plan, speculate, and attempt to gain control over our forthcoming experiences. While a degree of foresight is essential for effective decision-making and goal-setting, an excessive fixation on the future can lead to a range of challenges that affect our ability to live mindfully in the present.

One significant consequence of being overly preoccupied with the future is that it can lead us to overlook the richness and potential of the present moment. When our attention is consistently directed towards what might come next, we run the risk of missing out on the opportunities, experiences, and beauty that surround us in the here and now. This constant mental projection into the future can hinder our ability to fully engage with our immediate surroundings, relationships, and activities.

Additionally, the intense focus on the future can give rise to heightened levels of anxiety and stress. The uncertainty and unpredictability of what lies ahead can evoke worries, doubts, and concerns about potential outcomes. As we ruminate about future events, our minds become entangled in a web of "what ifs" and hypothetical scenarios, diverting our attention from the current moment and contributing to a sense of restlessness.

This forward-looking orientation can also lead to a sense of dissatisfaction with the present. By habitually comparing the current state to our envisioned future, we may develop an attitude that devalues our present circumstances. This mindset, rooted in the belief that fulfillment lies solely in what is yet to come, can breed a sense of discontent and prevent us from fully embracing the inherent value of our current situation.

This tendency to focus on the future can also serve as a means of escaping from uncomfortable emotions or challenges in the present. The anticipation of better times ahead can be soothing, providing a mental refuge from difficult feelings. However, relying on the future as a perpetual source of comfort prevents us from addressing our emotions constructively and inhibits our personal growth and resilience.

Ultimately, striking a balance between considering the future and being present in the moment is essential. Mindfulness practices remind us to acknowledge thoughts about the future without being consumed by them. By grounding ourselves in the present, we can make more thoughtful decisions, cultivate a deeper appreciation for our current circumstances, and effectively manage the fluctuations of the monkey mind. Recognizing the potential drawbacks of excessive future-focused thinking empowers us to foster a harmonious relationship between planning for the future and embracing the richness of the present moment.

> ***"The secret of health for both mind and body is not to mourn for the past, worry about the future, or anticipate troubles, but to live in the present moment wisely and earnestly."***
>
> **– *Buddha***

The art of Mindful Living involves cultivating an open and non-judgmental awareness of our thoughts, emotions, sensations, and surroundings. By observing these aspects without attempting to control or suppress them, we create a space for inner calm and self-understanding to flourish.

At the core of this practice lies the recognition of the monkey mind's tendency and addressing this challenge by embracing the present moment and engage with it wholeheartedly. This practice is grounded because the present is the only reality we truly have, and by living in alignment with it, we can experience a deeper sense of contentment and clarity.

The power of living in the present lies in its ability to free us from the shackles of past regrets and future

anxieties. This explores how our attachment to experiences and our anticipation of future events often rob us of the opportunity to fully experience the richness of the now. The relentless curiosity about the future can obscure the beauty and potential inherent in the present moment, causing us to miss out on life's simple pleasures.

Mindfulness acts as a guide, helping us develop the capacity to observe our thoughts and emotions with detachment, allowing us to redirect our attention from the monkey mind's wandering.

12

SETTING BOUNDARIES AND SAYING 'NO'

In "The Power of Habit", Duhigg delves into the principles closely related to the idea of saying "no" and making intentional choices.

Duhigg emphasizes the concept of the habit loop, which consists of a cue, a routine, and a reward. He explains that by recognizing the cues that trigger our habits and the rewards we seek, we can intentionally change our routines to establish healthier habits. This concept can be applied to the act of saying "no" as well.

Cue: In saying "yes" to every request or opportunity, the cue might be the fear of missing out (FOMO), societal pressure to be agreeable, or the desire to please others.

Routine: The routine here is saying "yes" to everything without considering the consequences or your own priorities.

Reward: The reward could be short-term gratification, praise from others, or the avoidance of conflict.

By applying the principles from "The Power of Habit," you can reframe your habit loop:

Cue: Recognize the cues that prompt you to say "yes" reflexively. Is it societal pressure, a fear of disappointing others, or the need to feel busy all the time?

Routine: Instead of automatically saying "yes," you can choose to insert a new routine, which is the act of saying "no" or at least pausing to evaluate the request.

Reward: Understand the long-term rewards of saying "no." It might mean more time for your personal goals, reduced stress, or better work-life balance.

By consciously reprogramming your habit loop in this manner, and reaffirms the idea that saying "no" is not about denying opportunities but about choosing the right ones that genuinely benefit your life.

BUT WHY SAYING 'NO' IS THAT IMPORTANT IN LIFE?

In a world where the culture of saying "yes" to every opportunity is often celebrated, advocating for the ability to say "no" may seem unconventional. However, saying "no" is not only important but also essential for our overall well-being, personal growth, and success.

Foremost, saying "no" is a crucial way to preserve your time and energy. Think of your time and energy as limited resources, much like money in your bank account. When you constantly say "yes" to every request or opportunity that comes your way, you are essentially spending these valuable resources without careful consideration. This can lead to exhaustion, burnout, and a sense of being overwhelmed. Burnout, in particular, can have detrimental effects on your physical and mental health, reducing your overall productivity and increasing stress levels. By saying "no" selectively, you can safeguard your time and energy for the things that truly matter to you, enabling you to maintain a healthier work-life balance.

Furthermore, saying "no" is a powerful tool for setting clear boundaries. Establishing boundaries is essential for maintaining healthy relationships and self-respect. Saying "no" in a respectful yet firm manner helps define your limits and communicates to others what is acceptable and what is not. This fosters healthier and more respectful interactions with others.

Additionally, saying "no" allows you to prioritize your goals effectively. Life is filled with a multitude of opportunities, distractions, and commitments. If you say "yes" to all of them, you risk spreading yourself too thin, diluting your efforts across various activities, and potentially neglecting your core objectives. By judiciously saying "no" to less important or distracting opportunities, you can channel your time and energy toward what truly aligns with your goals and values. This focused approach increases your chances of success and fulfillment in areas that matter most to you.

> ***"Saying 'no' to the unnecessary is saying 'yes' to the essential."***

Moreover, saying "no" is an act of self-care. By saying "no" when necessary, you can allocate time for rest, relaxation, and activities that rejuvenate and restore you. This contributes to your overall resilience and ability to cope with life's demands.

Lastly, saying "no" is instrumental in building and maintaining respect and integrity. If you consistently say "yes" to commitments or requests but cannot fulfill them because of overextension, others may perceive you as unreliable or inconsistent. Saying "no" when it is warranted demonstrates honesty and integrity. It communicates that you take your commitments seriously and that your word can be trusted. This enhances your reputation and strengthens your relationships.

> ***"Boundaries are not walls; they are bridges to self-respect and well-being."***

Imagine boundaries as invisible lines that are not meant to keep people out but to define a space where we can thrive, feel safe, and be true to ourselves.

In relationships, for instance, boundaries act as bridges that facilitate healthy interactions. They are like unspoken agreements that say, "This is how I expect to be treated, and this is how I will treat you in return." These agreements create a foundation of respect, trust, and understanding. They allow us to express our needs, desires, and limits without fear of judgment or rejection and create an environment where our self-respect can flourish.

Boundaries also serve as bridges to well-being. They enable us to protect our physical and emotional health. For example, setting boundaries around work hours ensures that we have time for self-care, rest, and relaxation. This contributes to our overall well-being by preventing burnout and stress.

Boundaries are not barriers that isolate us; instead, they are bridges that connect us with others while preserving our self-respect and well-being. They foster healthier relationships, protect our emotional and physical health, and guide us toward a more balanced and fulfilling life.

To explain the point further, let's delve into a short story of Sudhir who unlocked the power of saying "No".

Sudhir was ambitious, hardworking, and always eager to help others. Sudhir's kindness was well- known, and he often found himself saying "yes" to every favor, request, and opportunity that came his way. His days were filled with commitments to friends, colleagues, and acquaintances, leaving him with little time for his own dreams and aspirations.

Sudhir had a dream that burned brightly within him—to start his own tech company. He had a brilliant idea for a software application that could revolutionize the industry. However, his constant "yes" to others had pushed this dream to the back burner. Every time he thought about pursuing it, someone else's request would pull him away.

One day, Sudhir received a phone call that would change everything. It was a childhood friend, Raj, who had just started a new business venture. Raj needed Sudhir's technical expertise to develop a crucial software module that would make or break his company. Raj was desperate, and his request was heartfelt. Sudhir couldn't bear to see his old friend in distress, so he agreed to help.

Days turned into weeks, and Sudhir dedicated himself entirely to Raj's project. He worked tirelessly, often sacrificing sleep and personal time to meet tight deadlines. As the project progressed, Sudhir's own dreams seemed more distant than ever. He watched as Raj's company began to thrive, while his own vision slipped further away. One evening, Sudhir sat alone in his dimly lit apartment, pondering the choices he had made. His dream was fading into the background, and he felt a sense of frustration and regret. He realized that his inability to say "no" was robbing him of the life he had envisioned.

The turning point came when Sudhir received an invitation to a tech innovation conference. This event was a rare opportunity to showcase his own idea and secure potential investors. However, it coincided with a crucial phase in Raj's project. The choice was agonizing, but Sudhir knew he had to make a decision that would define his future.

With a heavy heart, Sudhir called Raj and explained his situation honestly. He expressed his desire to attend the conference and finally pursue his own dream. To his surprise, Raj understood. He told Sudhir that he had always known about Sudhir's entrepreneurial spirit and encouraged him to go.

At the conference, Sudhir presented his idea with passion and conviction. His innovation garnered significant interest, and he soon found investors willing to support his vision. The sacrifices he had made in the past had not been in vain; they had led him to this moment.

Over time, Sudhir's tech company grew and thrived, becoming a household name in the industry. Raj's venture also succeeded, and the two friends remained close, supporting each other's achievements.

Sudhir had learned a valuable lesson on his journey to success - the power of saying "no." By making the difficult choice to prioritize his own dreams over immediate obligations, he had unlocked a future full of possibilities. Sudhir realized that saying "no" when necessary was not selfish but a path to achieving his true potential.

Sudhir's experience is not unique; these principles hold universal significance in our lives for several reasons:

> ***"In the art of saying 'no,' we find the canvas to paint the masterpiece of our lives."***

This topic can also be explored further from Vedic Philosophy particularly in texts like the Bhagavad Gita and Upanishads, These teachings can be related to the importance of saying "no" and setting boundaries.

UNDERSTANDING THE SELF

Vedic philosophy encourages individuals to understand their true self or atman. The atman is considered eternal and unchanging, distinct from the transient physical body and the ever-changing mind. By recognizing the eternal nature of the self, individuals can gain insight into their core values, desires, and purpose in life.

This understanding of the self relates to saying "no" because it prompts individuals to align their actions with their inner values and authentic self. Saying "no" when necessary becomes an act of honoring one's true self, avoiding actions or commitments that go against their fundamental nature and purpose.

DHARMA AND DUTY

Dharma, often translated as duty or righteousness, is a central concept in Vedic philosophy. It refers to the moral and ethical duties that each person is obligated to fulfill based on their role in society, stage of life (ashrama), and personal disposition (guna).

Saying "no" can be seen as an expression of dharma. When individuals say "no" to requests or commitments that would conflict with their dharma, they are adhering to their ethical responsibilities. Setting boundaries is a way of upholding one's dharma and maintaining balance in fulfilling their duties.

BALANCING MATERIAL AND SPIRITUAL PURSUITS

Vedic philosophy acknowledges the importance of balancing material and spiritual pursuits in life. While fulfilling material obligations is necessary, it is equally crucial to dedicate time to spiritual growth and self- realization.

Saying "no" can help individuals strike this balance. By setting boundaries around their time and energy, they can ensure they have the space for spiritual practices, self- reflection, and personal growth. In this way, saying "no" becomes a means of prioritizing spiritual well-being alongside material responsibilities.

Mahatma Gandhi's quote, "A 'no' uttered from the deepest conviction is better than a 'yes' merely uttered to please, or worse, to avoid trouble," encapsulates the essence of authenticity and moral integrity.

When Gandhi speaks of a "no" uttered from the deepest conviction, he is referring to a refusal or dissent that arises from a profound and genuine belief. It signifies the courage to stand firm in the face of opposition or adversity, even when it's challenging.

Conversely, Gandhi contrasts this with a "yes" offered merely to please others or avoid trouble. This kind of agreement is often driven by external pressures, the fear of conflict, or a desire to conform to societal expectations. While it may temporarily smooth over disagreements or maintain a sense of harmony, it lacks the depth and honesty of a "no" grounded in conviction.

This perspective carries profound implications for our lives. It encourages us to be discerning and deliberate in our choices, to assess whether our decisions align with our core values and beliefs. It reminds us that even when faced with opposition or potential consequences, speaking our truth is a powerful act of moral courage.

> ***"Saying 'no' doesn't make you negative; it makes you selective."***

Let's explore the dynamics of why a person who habitually says "yes" to everything may be perceived as emotionally weak compared to someone who confidently says "no" with conviction and is seen as trustworthy.

When an individual frequently responds with a "yes" to every request or demand, it often indicates a deep-seated fear of disapproval or rejection. This fear can stem from a lack of self-confidence or a desire to maintain harmony in their relationships. They may worry that declining requests will lead to conflict or a negative perception by others. Consequently, they tend to acquiesce to avoid confrontation or the possibility of being seen as uncooperative.

Over time, this pattern of always saying "yes" can lead to over commitment. These individuals find themselves taking on more responsibilities and obligations than they can reasonably manage. This overextension can erode their emotional well-being and self-esteem, further reinforcing the perception of emotional weakness.

In contrast, someone who confidently says "no" with conviction does so because they have a strong sense of their own boundaries and priorities. Their ability to decline requests when necessary demonstrates that they respect their own limitations and are not easily swayed by external pressures. This conviction in saying "no" indicates that they can be trusted for their words and actions. When they do say "yes," it carries more weight and reliability because it is a deliberate and thoughtful choice.

> ***"Saying 'no' is not negativity; it's wisdom in prioritizing what truly matters."***

Saying "no" to things does not make someone a negative person. Instead, it reflects their ability to prioritize efficiently and make intentional choices. This distinction is important because it highlights the positive aspects of setting boundaries and making thoughtful decisions.

> ***"Life without boundaries is like a ship without a rudder, adrift in a sea of chaos."***

This metaphor vividly captures the significance of boundaries in our lives. Just as a ship's rudder steers it through the unpredictable waters of the sea, boundaries provide us with direction, purpose, and a sense of worth in the unpredictable journey of life.

1. DIRECTION AND PURPOSE

Boundaries act as our navigational tools, helping us define the limits of our personal, emotional, and social spaces. They give us a clear sense of direction by guiding our choices and actions. Without boundaries, life can feel aimless, as we lack the guidance needed to make intentional decisions that align with our goals and values. Boundaries provide the framework within which we can pursue our passions and aspirations, giving life meaning and purpose.

2. SELF-RESPECT AND SELF-WORTH

Boundaries are a declaration of self-respect. When we establish and maintain boundaries, we communicate to ourselves and others that our needs, values, and well-being matter. This affirmation of self-worth is essential for healthy self-esteem. Without boundaries, we risk diminishing our self-worth as we may compromise our values or allow others to disregard our needs, eroding our sense of self-respect.

3. PROTECTION FROM CHAOS AND OVERWHELM

Life can be chaotic and overwhelming, much like the unpredictable sea. Boundaries act as protective barriers, shielding us from the excesses and intrusions that can lead to stress and burnout. They help us manage our time, energy, and resources effectively, preventing us from becoming lost in the tumultuous currents of life.

4. HEALTHY RELATIONSHIPS

Boundaries are crucial for building and maintaining healthy relationships. They define the limits of acceptable behavior and interactions in relationships. Without boundaries, relationships can become strained as individuals may unintentionally cross each other's boundaries. Healthy boundaries foster respect, trust, and understanding, enhancing the quality of our connections with others.

5. EMPOWERMENT AND CONTROL

Boundaries empower us to take control of our lives. They allow us to make deliberate choices that align with our values and goals, rather than succumbing to external pressures or the whims of others. This sense of empowerment contributes to our sense of worth and self- efficacy.

Boundaries are not restrictions on our freedom but the essential tools that provide direction, protect our well-being, and affirm our self-worth in the complex voyage of life. Without boundaries, we risk drifting aimlessly, encountering chaos, and losing sight of our worth and purpose. Establishing and respecting boundaries is a powerful means of navigating life's challenges with clarity, intentionality, and a strong sense of self-worth.

> ***"Always be open to opportunities but stay away from opportunists by saying no."***

It encapsulates a wise approach to navigating life's diverse offerings and interactions. It underscores the importance of striking a balance between receptivity to positive opportunities and the need to protect oneself from those who might exploit or manipulate.

Being open to opportunities is an admirable quality. It signifies a mindset of curiosity, growth, and a willingness to explore new horizons. Such openness often leads to personal and professional development, as individuals are more likely to learn, adapt, and evolve when they embrace the possibilities that come their way.

However, the quote also recognizes the need for discern-ment and boundary-setting. While embracing opportunities is valuable, it is equally important to exercise caution and discretion. Not everyone who presents an opportunity has pure intentions, and some individuals may try to take advantage of your openness or goodwill for their own benefit.

In such cases, saying "no" becomes an essential tool in protecting your interests and well-being. It is a declaration of your boundaries and a refusal to be manipulated or exploited. It ensures that you maintain control over your choices and decisions, rather than being swayed by the agendas of opportunists.

Moreover, saying "no" to opportunists is an act of self- respect and self-preservation. It safeguards your time, energy, and resources, allowing you to allocate them to pursuits and relationships that genuinely align with your values and goals. It prevents the erosion of your autonomy and integrity.

It urges individuals to maintain their openness to opportunities while also recognizing the importance of setting boundaries and discerning the true nature of those who present these opportunities. By doing so, individuals can navigate the complexities of life with resilience, integrity, and a commitment to their own well-being.

"Saying 'no' is not a limitation; it's the key to unlocking your priorities."

13

THE JOY OF GIVING: ACTS OF KINDNESS AND THEIR RIPPLE EFFECT

In the bustling city of Mumbai, where the cacophony of traffic and chatter filled the air, there stood a humble tea stall named "Chai Sipper." The owner, Sudeep, was not only known for his fragrant masala chai but also for his generous spirit. He had a heart as warm as the steaming cups he served to his customers.

One crisp winter morning, as Sudeep was setting up his stall, he noticed a frail old man named Ram shivering near the stall's counter. Ram was a regular visitor, often buying a cup of chai to keep warm. Without a second thought, Sudeep handed Ram a cup of chai and a freshly baked samosa.

Tears welled up in Ram's eyes as he accepted Sudeep's gift. "Bless you, my son," he whispered, his voice quivering.

Sudeep smiled warmly and replied, "You're welcome, Ram Ji. Stay warm today."

Little did he know that this simple act of kindness would set off a chain reaction of goodwill that would touch the lives of many.

As the weeks passed, Sudeep's daily act of kindness toward Ram became a talk of the neighborhood. Customers at "Chai Sipper" began bringing warm clothes, blankets, and hot meals for Ram. The community of kindness was forming around Sudeep's initial act.

One day, a young woman named Ahana, inspired by Sudeep's generosity, decided to organize a clothing drive in her college. Word spread, and soon, the entire city was involved. Ram, now wearing donated winter clothes, felt a warmth he hadn't known in years, both from the garments and the love of his newfound community.

The ripple effect continued to grow. "Chai Sipper" became a hub of compassion, where people not only enjoyed chai but also shared stories of their own acts of kindness. Sudeep began organizing community events, such as food drives and free tutoring sessions for underprivileged children, which further strengthened the bonds between neighbors.

One of Sudeep's regular customers, Maya, a retired teacher, volunteered her time to teach basic literacy skills to Ram and others in similar situations. Local businesses started offering job opportunities to those who had once been overlooked. Ram's life was changing, and he had hope for a brighter future.

The city's spirit of giving extended far beyond "Chai Sipper." Acts of kindness became a way of life in the community. People would share meals with strangers, help the homeless find shelter, and support local charities. The city had become a place where everyone felt valued and loved.

One evening, as the sun set over Mumbai, Sudeep gazed at his bustling tea stall, his heart full of gratitude for the beautiful transformation that had taken place. It all began with a simple act of kindness to an old man named Ram, a single drop that had created ripples of joy throughout the city.

As the years passed, the legacy of Sudeep's kindness continued to thrive, reminding everyone that the joy of giving was a gift that kept on giving. And so, in Mumbai, the city where love and kindness flowed like a river, the cycle of giving and receiving continued, perpetuating the beautiful ripple effect of goodwill for generations to come.

"Acts of kindness are the seeds we sow; their ripple effect grows into a garden of love and compassion."

In life, each one of us holds the power to sow seeds of kindness. Like a gardener tending to a garden, we nurture these acts of goodness in the fertile soil of our daily interactions. These seeds may appear small, inconspicuous even, but their potential is vast and transformative.

Imagine, if you will, a garden. Not just any garden, but a garden of the soul—a garden where the seeds of kindness are sown. This garden is tended by the hands of ordinary people, people like you and me, who understand that even the simplest acts of kindness can have a profound impact.

As we plant these seeds of kindness, they take root and begin to grow. The first tender shoots emerge as smiles exchanged between strangers on a crowded street. A door held open; a cup of coffee bought for the person behind you in line—these are the early signs of growth in our garden.

Further in, beneath the shade of a wise old tree, the seeds of generosity begin to flourish. These are the acts that go beyond the superficial, the ones that require a bit of sacrifice—a meal shared with a hungry soul, a coat given to someone shivering in the cold. In this part of the garden, we find warmth and interconnectedness.

Then, as we continue along the path, we encounter the seeds of compassion. Here, the acts of kindness are deeply rooted in empathy and understanding. It's about lending a hand to someone struggling with their burdens, offering a shoulder to lean on in times of sorrow, or simply being present for a friend in need. In this part of the garden, we learn the true meaning of empathy.

What's remarkable about this garden is that it's not confined to any place. It's not just your garden or mine; it's a collective garden nurtured by humanity. The beauty of it lies because it knows no boundaries. It grows in cities and villages, across cultures and continents, and even in the most unexpected corners of the world.

The most wondrous thing about this garden is that it doesn't stop growing. When you sow a seed of kindness, it doesn't just end with that one act. It has the power to multiply, creating a ripple effect that extends far beyond your immediate surroundings. Just as one flower's bloom can inspire others to burst into color, your acts of kindness can inspire more acts of kindness.

In giving, we receive the most precious gift of all—a heart overflowing with the joy of making a difference.

In the realm of literature, the profound truth that "in giving, we receive the most precious gift of all" finds a poignant resonance. Let's journey into the world of literature to explore this idea through the lens of one of the most beloved authors of all time, Charles Dickens, and his timeless classic, "A Christmas Carol".

As the story unfolds, we are introduced to the miserly Ebenezer Scrooge, a character known for his relentless pursuit of wealth and indifference to the suffering of others. He is a man whose heart has grown cold and distant, much like the winters that envelope London in Dickens' tale. Scrooge's life revolves around the acquisition of material riches, and he shows no inclination towards the plight of the poor or the joys of human connection.

However, as the story progresses, we see a transformation in Scrooge that is nothing short of miraculous. It all begins on a cold Christmas Eve when he is visited by the ghost of his former business partner, Jacob Marley, who is condemned to wander the earth weighed down by heavy chains forged from a lifetime of selfishness and greed. Marley's visit serves as a warning to Scrooge about the path he is on.

But it is the subsequent visitation by the three spirits—the Ghosts of Christmas Past, Present, and Yet to Come—that truly awakens Scrooge's dormant humanity. Through these spectral encounters, he is confronted with the consequences of his actions and the suffering of those he has neglected, including his own impoverished clerk, Bob Cratchit, and Cratchit's ailing son, Tiny Tim.

As Scrooge witnesses the Cratchit family's humble Christmas celebration and Tiny Tim's uncertain fate, his heart begins to thaw. He is overcome with empathy and a newfound understanding of the value of giving and sharing. The Ghost of Christmas Present, in particular, shows Scrooge the joy and warmth that can be found giving, even when one has little to give.

Upon awakening from his harrowing night of ghostly visits, Scrooge is a changed man. He is filled with a burning desire to make amends for his past behavior and to embrace the spirit of generosity. He donates to charity, provides a feast for the Cratchit family, and becomes a second father to Tiny Tim.

In the end, the most remarkable transformation in Scrooge is not his newfound wealth or his social standing but the profound change that has taken place in his heart. His joy and fulfillment come not from hoarding his wealth but from the joy of making a difference in the lives of others, especially in the life of Tiny Tim. He discovers that giving, in its truest sense, is the most precious gift of all—a gift that fills the heart with warmth, compassion, and the indescribable joy of knowing that one has made a positive impact on the world.

Dickens' "A Christmas Carol" beautifully illustrates the timeless wisdom that in giving, we receive. Scrooge's transformation serves as a reminder that the act of giving not only enriches the lives of others but also nourishes our own souls, leaving us with hearts overflowing with the joy of making a difference in the world.

> ***"When we give from the heart, we not only brighten someone's day but also light the path for others to follow."***

The essence of this sentiment can be beautifully illustrated through the life and legacy of Mother Teresa, whose selfless dedication to serving others left an indelible mark on the world.

Born as Agnes Gonxha Bojaxhiu in Skopje, North Macedonia, Mother Teresa felt a deep calling to dedicate her life to helping the poorest of the poor. She left her home at a young age to join the Sisters of Loreto, a religious community in Ireland. After several years of teaching and nursing, she experienced a powerful inner calling within her vocation.

In 1948, she left the convent and moved to the slums of Calcutta (now Kolkata), India, where she started her mission to care for the destitute and dying. With unwavering devotion, she began by providing a simple, clean place for people to die with dignity. She and her fellow sisters would venture out into the streets to pick up those who had been abandoned, offering them love, care, and a compassionate presence in their final moments.

As she tirelessly worked to alleviate the suffering of others, Mother Teresa lived a life devoid of personal comfort or luxury. She embraced poverty and simplicity, choosing to identify with the very people she served. Her actions spoke volumes about her commitment to living for others.

Over the decades, Mother Teresa's selfless service to the poor and the dying touched the hearts of people worldwide. She became a global symbol of compassion, inspiring countless individuals to take up the cause of helping the less fortunate.

Yet, it wasn't just her life that left an indelible mark; it was her legacy. When Mother Teresa passed away in 1997, people from all walks of life mourned her loss. Her funeral was attended by world leaders, dignitaries, and countless ordinary people who had been touched by her work. They cried not only for her passing but for the profound impact she had made on the world.

Mother Teresa's legacy serves as a testament to the fact that when we dedicate ourselves to the service of others, our influence transcends our earthly existence, and people remember us not for our possessions but for the love and kindness we shared with the world.

In Hindu mythology, the concept of giving, known as "Daan" or "Dana," holds great significance and is deeply intertwined with the principles of dharma (duty or righteousness), karma (action and its consequences), and seva (selfless service). The joy of giving in Hinduism is seen as a noble and virtuous act that not only benefits the recipient but also uplifts the giver's spiritual and moral well-being. Several stories and teachings from Hindu mythology emphasize the importance of giving and its positive effects:

1. **Lord Krishna and Sudama:** One of the most famous stories in Hindu mythology revolves around Lord Krishna and his childhood friend, Sudama. Sudama was a poor Brahmin who visited Lord Krishna with a simple gift of rice flakes. Despite his dire circumstances, Sudama gave his humble offering with pure devotion and love. In return, Lord Krishna blessed Sudama with prosperity and riches. This story illustrates that even a small and heartfelt gift can bring great blessings.
2. **The Story of King Harishchandra:** King Harishchandra is revered for his unwavering commitment to truth and righteousness. His story teaches the importance of giving, even in the face of extreme adversity. Harishchandra gave away his kingdom, wealth, and even his own family to fulfill his promises. Through his sacrifices and acts of charity, he ultimately attained salvation.
3. **Lord Shiva and the Poor Beggar:** In another tale, Lord Shiva and Goddess Parvati disguised themselves as

beggars and visited the home of a poor Brahmin couple. Despite their poverty, the couple offered the beggars a simple meal. Pleased by their selflessness, Lord Shiva revealed his true form and blessed them with prosperity.

4. **The Story of King Rantideva:** King Rantideva is known for his selfless giving, even during times of extreme hunger and hardship. He never turned away anyone who sought his help, even when he had nothing left to give. His story emphasizes the virtue of compassion and the joy of giving, no matter one's circumstances.

In Hinduism, giving is considered a sacred duty, and it is believed that acts of charity lead to spiritual growth and purification. These stories from Hindu mythology serve as timeless reminders that generosity, kindness, and selfless service bring both worldly and spiritual rewards, enriching the lives of both givers and recipients.

> ***"Karma's ledger records our deeds, but it's the ledger of the heart that truly defines our legacy through selfless giving."***

Once, in the sacred town of Varanasi, nestled on the banks of the holy Ganges River, there lived a devout man named Arjun. He was a firm believer in the concept of karma and the idea that one's actions shape their destiny.

Arjun was known throughout the town for his unwavering commitment to selfless giving. He would rise before the sun, fill a basket with freshly cooked meals, and set off on a daily pilgrimage to the nearby slums, where the poorest of the poor resided.

As he walked through the narrow, dusty lanes, he would offer food to hungry children, provide blankets to shivering elders, and share his meager possessions with those in need. His acts of kindness knew no bounds, and he did not seek recognition or praise for his deeds.

One scorching summer afternoon, Arjun encountered a beggar sitting by the roadside. The man's emaciated form and parched lips spoke of days without food or water. Arjun, without hesitation, offered him his water flask and the meager meal he had carried for himself that day.

The beggar, his eyes filled with gratitude, asked Arjun, "Why do you do this, my friend? Why do you give so selflessly when you have so little yourself?"

Arjun smiled, his face weathered by years of devotion, and replied, "I believe in the power of karma. Every act of kindness we perform is like sowing a seed in the vast field of destiny. It may take time, but eventually, those seeds bear fruit. By giving selflessly today, I am sowing the seeds of a better tomorrow for myself and for those I help."

The beggar was deeply moved by Arjun's words. He realized that there was a profound connection between karma and selfless giving. Arjun's actions exemplified the idea that the energy one puts into the world comes back to them, either directly or indirectly, shaping their own life's journey.

Years passed, and Arjun continued his acts of selfless giving. He lived a simple life, never seeking riches or worldly success. Yet, his heart was content, for he knew that every meal he shared, every blanket he provided, and every smile he offered was a deposit in the bank of karma.

As time flowed like the sacred Ganges itself, Arjun's life bore witness to the interconnectedness of karma and selfless giving. People from all walks of life admired his compassion and joined him in his mission. The town of Varanasi itself transformed, becoming a place where generosity and kindness flowed like the holy waters of the Ganges.

THE SCIENCE OF KINDNESS

In recent years, scientific research has provided interesting evidence that acts of kindness and generosity have a profound impact on both the giver and the recipient.

The Release of "Feel-Good" Chemicals: Often referred to as the "love hormone" or "bonding hormone," oxytocin is released when individuals engage in acts of kindness, particularly those involving social bonding and trust. This hormone is associated with feelings of connection and empathy. Acts of kindness, such as helping others or donating to charity, can trigger the release of endorphins. These natural chemicals are known for their ability to promote feelings of happiness and reduce stress and pain.

The Impact on Stress Reduction: Kindness has been linked to decreased levels of the stress hormone cortisol. Engaging in acts of generosity can help individuals manage stress and anxiety more effectively.

Enhancement of Emotional Well-being: Numerous studies have demonstrated that those who engage in regular acts of kindness tend to report higher levels of life satisfaction and overall happiness.

Improved Physical Health: Acts of kindness have been associated with improved cardiovascular health. The positive emotions generated by giving can lead to lower blood pressure and reduced risk of heart disease. Some studies suggest that individuals who engage in acts of kindness may experience increased longevity. Acts of giving and altruism have been associated with a lower risk of mortality. Engaging in acts of kindness may lead to positive changes in brain structure and function, enhancing empathy, compassion, and emotional resilience.

Strengthening Social Connections: Kindness fosters social bonds and positive interactions. Engaging in altruistic acts can lead to the formation of new friendships, strengthen existing relationships, and create a sense of community and create a kindness loop.

Boosting Self-esteem and Self-worth: Acts of kindness can enhance an individual's self- esteem and self-worth. When people see the positive impact they have on others, it reinforces their sense of value and purpose.

The science of kindness reinforces the idea that kindness is not just a virtue; it is a fundamental aspect of human nature that is deeply ingrained in our biology and psychology.

Now the question that may arise would be who doesn't want to spread joy of giving but still many of us are not doing it. But why? So, let's discuss hurdles and barriers that many of us face and what are the reasons?

CHALLENGES AND BARRIERS

In the pursuit of acts of kindness and giving, several challenges and barriers can emerge, potentially hindering individuals and communities from fully embracing these practices.

Self-centeredness often stands as a formidable barrier. In a society that frequently emphasizes individualism and self-interest, many individuals find it challenging to shift their focus from self to others. Overcoming this innate self-centeredness can be an ongoing struggle.

Another significant hurdle is the fear of exploitation. Some individuals hesitate to engage in acts of kindness because of concerns that their generosity may be taken advantage of or manipulated by others. This fear can lead to hesitancy in giving and sharing.

Resource limitations can also be a significant obstacle. When individuals have limited financial or material resources, they may struggle to provide assistance or support to others, even when they have the intention to do so. Meeting their basic needs may take precedence.

Time constraints represent another challenge. Busy schedules and demanding responsibilities can leave individuals with limited time to engage in acts of kindness or volunteer work. Finding a balance between personal and altruistic commitments can be a real challenge.

Compassion fatigue, a condition characterized by emotional exhaustion and reduced empathetic capacity, can affect those regularly involved in caregiving or humanitarian work. This exhaustion can lead to a diminished capacity to continue acts of kindness consistently.

Overcoming these challenges and barriers requires a combination of self-awareness, community support, and a commitment to cultivating a culture of kindness. Recognizing these obstacles is the first step in finding effective strategies to address them, ultimately fostering a more compassionate and giving society.

HOW TO OVERCOME THESE CHALLENGES?

While challenges and barriers to acts of kindness may arise, there are strategies and approaches that individuals and communities can employ to overcome these obstacles and promote a culture of giving and compassion.

1. CULTIVATE SELF-AWARENESS

Recognize and acknowledge personal biases, fears, or self-centered tendencies that may hinder acts of kindness. Self-awareness is the first step in addressing these barriers.

2. START SMALL

Begin with manageable acts of kindness. Small gestures, such as holding the door for someone or offering a smile, can gradually build the habit of giving.

3. EDUCATE AND RAISE AWARENESS

Promote awareness about the benefits of acts of kindness and the positive impact they have on individuals and communities. Education can inspire more people to engage in giving.

4. FOSTER A SUPPORTIVE COMMUNITY

Surround yourself with like-minded individuals who value kindness and altruism. Communities and social networks that encourage giving can provide encouragement and motivation.

5. SET REALISTIC EXPECTATIONS

Understand that acts of kindness need not be grand or resource-intensive. Setting realistic expectations for what you can give within your means can alleviate the pressure to do more than you can comfortably manage.

6. PRIORITIZE TIME MANAGEMENT

Efficiently manage your time by setting aside specific moments for acts of kindness or volunteering. Prioritizing these activities in your schedule can help overcome time constraints.

7. SEEK GUIDANCE AND RESOURCES

Reach out to organizations and resources that facilitate acts of kindness and volunteering. These organizations can provide guidance, opportunities, and resources for those looking to give back.

8. PRACTICE SELF-CARE

Avoid compassion fatigue and burnout by practicing self-care. Ensure that you take time to recharge and maintain your emotional well-being.

9. ENCOURAGE TRUST-BUILDING

Foster an environment of trust and mutual respect within your community. Building trust can help alleviate fears of exploitation or manipulation.

10. LEAD BY EXAMPLE

Be a role model for acts of kindness. When others witness your generosity and compassion, it can inspire them to follow suit.

11. PROMOTE A CULTURE OF KINDNESS

Advocate for kindness initiatives within your workplace, school, or community. Encourage policies and practices that support and celebrate acts of kindness.

12. REFLECT ON MOTIVES

Regularly reflect on your motives for giving. Ensure that your acts of kindness are driven by genuine compassion and a desire to make a positive impact.

By employing these strategies and approaches, individuals and communities can navigate and overcome the challenges and barriers that may arise in their pursuit of acts of kindness. Over time, these efforts can contribute to a more compassionate and giving society.

14

THE ROLE OF MENTORSHIP: LEARNING FROM OTHERS' WISDOM

Learning from our own experiences is an essential part of personal growth and development. It involves navigating life's challenges, making decisions, and facing the consequences of our actions. This process, however, comes with some inherent limitations.

However, our experiences are inherently limited to our own lives. We only encounter a subset of the world's possibilities and challenges. Depending exclusively on our personal experiences may lead to a narrow perspective, causing us to miss out on valuable insights and innovative solutions that others have discovered.

This is where the concept of mentorship comes into play. Mentorship involves seeking guidance and wisdom from experienced individuals who have already walked the path you wish to follow. It offers several advantages over relying solely on personal experience.

Firstly, mentors can provide valuable insights and knowledge that they have accumulated over their years of experience. This can significantly shorten the learning curve, allowing you to benefit from their expertise without having to make all the same mistakes they did and help mitigate the risks. By learning from someone who has already faced and overcome obstacles in your chosen field, you can avoid making costly errors and minimize the potential negative consequences of your actions.

Seeking mentorship from experienced individuals allows you to tap into their knowledge, gain a broader perspective, and reduce risks, making it a wise choice for personal and professional growth.

> ***"Mentorship is the bridge between inspiration and transformation."***

MENTORSHIP IN HISTORY AND CULTURE

Mentorship can trace its roots back to ancient civilizations. In ancient Greece, the concept of mentorship was introduced through Homer's epic poem, "The Odyssey". In this epic, Mentor was a trusted friend of Odysseus and was tasked with educating and guiding Odysseus's son, Telemachus, during his father's absence. This character became the archetype for the mentor figure, and the term "mentor" eventually came to represent a wise and experienced advisor or guide.

Throughout history, mentorship was often a formalized process within guilds and apprenticeship systems. Craftsmen, artists, and tradespeople passed down their knowledge and skills to the next generation through mentorship. This ensured the preservation of specialized knowledge and craftsmanship.

In ancient Greece, philosophical mentorship played a pivotal role in the development of philosophical thought. For example, Socrates mentored Plato, and Plato, in turn, mentored Aristotle. These mentor-mentee relationships were fundamental in shaping Western philosophy, as they facilitated the transmission of ideas and philosophical traditions.

Religious and spiritual traditions have also placed a strong emphasis on mentorship. In Christianity, for instance, the concept of discipleship involves spiritual mentorship, where experienced individuals guide newcomers in their faith. Similar mentorship structures exist in Buddhism, Islam, and other major religions, often through the roles of monks, imams, or spiritual leaders.

In the world of arts and culture, mentorship has played a vital role. Renaissance artists like Leonardo da Vinci took on apprentices who learned their craft under their guidance. In literature, famous authors such as Charles Dickens and Ernest Hemingway had mentors or influencers who helped shape their writing styles and careers.

In recent history, mentorship has evolved into various formal and informal movements. The Big Brothers Big Sisters program, for instance, pairs adult mentors with young mentees in need of guidance and support. Corporate mentorship programs have also become commonplace, where experienced professionals mentor newcomers to help them navigate their careers.

Mentorship has had a profound impact on individuals and societies throughout history. It has been a means of passing down knowledge, preserving cultural traditions, and fostering personal and professional development to produce leaders, thinkers, artists, and innovators. Mentorship remains a powerful tool for personal and societal growth, emphasizing the enduring value of learning from the wisdom of those who have come before us.

There can various types of Mentors as well. Some are listed below:

Formal Mentors: Formal mentors are individuals who are officially assigned or designated as mentors within a structured mentorship program or organization. These programs are often found in educational institutions, workplaces, and nonprofit organizations. Formal mentors typically have specific responsibilities outlined by the mentorship program. They offer guidance, support, and knowledge to their mentees, focusing on predetermined goals or skill development. The mentor-mentee relationship is often time-limited and comes with clear expectations.

Informal Mentors: Informal mentors are mentors who provide guidance and support on an unofficial, voluntary basis. These mentors are often found in personal and professional networks, such as family, friends, or colleagues. Informal mentors offer guidance based on their own experiences and expertise. They may not have a formalized relationship or specific goals but provide mentorship organically. Informal mentors can be valuable sources of wisdom and advice in various aspects of life.

Peer Mentors: Peer mentors are individuals who are at a similar career or life stage as their mentees. They offer support and guidance based on their own experiences and shared challenges. Peer mentors provide a relatable perspective as they have recently faced similar situations. They offer emotional support, share strategies for success, and provide a sense of camaraderie. Peer mentorship is common in educational settings, professional associations, and support groups.

Reverse Mentors: Reverse mentors are younger or less experienced individuals who provide mentorship to older or more senior individuals, often in the context of technology, social trends, or generational insights. Reverse mentors offer fresh perspectives and knowledge in areas where they have expertise. They bridge generational gaps and help senior mentees adapt to changing technologies and cultural shifts. This type of mentorship is increasingly relevant in today's fast-paced, tech- driven world.

Virtual Mentors: Virtual mentors are mentors who provide guidance and support through digital communication channels, such as email, video calls, or online platforms. Virtual mentors leverage technology to connect with mentees, making mentorship accessible regardless of geographical constraints. They provide advice, answer questions, and offer resources online. Virtual mentorship is valuable for remote or globally dispersed individuals seeking guidance.

> ***"In mentorship, the mentee is the canvas, and the mentor is the brush that paints the masterpiece of growth."***

HOW TO FIND A MENTOR WHO IS PERFECT FOR YOU?

Finding and selecting the right mentor is a deliberate and thoughtful process that involves many things. A well-matched mentor can provide invaluable guidance and support on your journey to personal and professional growth. Here are some key considerations and steps in finding and selecting the right mentor:

The first step in finding the right mentor is to clarify your goals and needs. Determine what specific skills, knowledge, or guidance you are seeking. Are you looking for career advancement, personal development, or industry-specific expertise? Understanding your objectives will help you narrow down the qualities and expertise you need in a mentor.

Networking is a valuable tool in mentorship. Start by tapping into your existing network. Consider friends, colleagues, professors, or acquaintances who may have the experience and insights you seek. Attend industry events, workshops, or seminars to expand your network and identify potential mentors. Additionally, research mentors in your field through online platforms, professional organizations, and social media to find individuals whose expertise aligns with your goals.

Compatibility is crucial in a mentor-mentee relationship. Your mentor should share your values, work ethic, and communication style. Evaluate potential mentors based on their experience, achievements, and reputation. Look for someone who has achieved what you aspire to accomplish and possesses the knowledge and skills you seek to acquire.

Reach out to trusted colleagues, professors, or professionals in your network for recommendations. Personal recommendations can help you identify mentors with a proven track record of mentorship success. Additionally, consider requesting references or testimonials from potential mentors to gain insights into their mentoring style and impact on previous mentees.

Once you've identified potential mentors, take the initiative to reach out. Craft a compelling and concise message explaining your objectives and why you believe they would be an excellent mentor. Express your genuine interest in learning from them. Building a rapport and demonstrating your commitment to the mentorship process can help you establish a strong connection.

Ensure that your prospective mentor has the time and willingness to commit to the mentorship relationship. Discuss expectations, such as the frequency and format of meetings, the duration of the mentorship, and the level of commitment required from both parties. Clarity on these aspects will help avoid misunderstandings later on.

In some cases, you may benefit from having multiple mentors with expertise in different areas relevant to your goals. These mentors can provide diverse perspectives and guidance. However, it's essential to manage these relationships effectively and ensure that they complement each other.

Once you've chosen a mentor, regularly assess the progress and effectiveness of the mentorship. Are you meeting your objectives? Is the relationship mutually beneficial? Effective mentorship should lead to tangible growth and development, and it's essential to communicate openly with your mentor about your expectations and any adjustments needed.

"A mentor is like a compass, guiding the mentee through uncharted waters, helping them navigate

the storms, and ultimately steering them towards the shores of wisdom and success."

THE IMPACT OF MENTORSHIP ON PERSONAL DEVELOPMENT

Mentorship has a profound and multifaceted impact on personal development. It serves as a catalyst for growth, offering individuals valuable guidance, support, and opportunities for self-improvement. In this exploration, we'll delve into how mentorship shapes personal development in various aspects of life.

Knowledge Transfer: Mentorship facilitates the transfer of knowledge and expertise from experienced mentors to mentees. Mentors share their insights, wisdom, and lessons learned from their own journeys. Whether in academic, professional, or life contexts, mentors provide a wealth of information that contributes to personal development.

Skill Development: Mentors often guide mentees in honing specific skills, whether technical, leadership, or communication-related. Through hands-on learning, constructive feedback, and practice, mentees gain proficiency and confidence in their abilities.

Networking and Opportunities: Mentors often introduce mentees to valuable networks, connections, and opportunities. Through mentorship, mentees gain access to a broader professional and social circle, increasing their chances of personal and career growth. Networking opportunities open doors to new experiences, collaborations, and potential mentors, further enriching the mentee's personal development journey.

Goal Setting and Accountability: Mentorship encourages goal setting and accountability. Mentors help mentees define clear objectives, create action plans, and track progress. This structured approach instills discipline and focus in the mentee's life, facilitating personal growth by turning aspirations into concrete achievements.

Emotional Support and Resilience: Mentorship provides emotional support during challenging times. Mentors offer a safe space for mentees to discuss concerns, seek advice, and receive guidance on personal issues. This emotional support enhances the mentee's resilience and coping mechanisms, enabling them to navigate life's ups and downs with greater fortitude.

Personal Growth and Self-Discovery: Mentorship encourages self-reflection and self-discovery. Mentors often challenge mentees to explore their values, beliefs, and aspirations. This introspection leads to personal growth by helping individuals better understand themselves, their goals, and their purpose in life.

Lifelong Learning and Adaptability: Mentorship fosters a culture of continuous learning and adaptability. Mentees learn not only from their mentors but also from observing their mentors' behavior and attitudes. This exposure to a growth mindset and a commitment to improvement encourages mentees to embrace lifelong learning and adapt to changing circumstances, contributing to ongoing personal development.

PAYING IT FORWARD

Life is a long journey of learning and it never ends. But the things that you have learnt, others need to learn them as well. It is necessary to pass on the baton or else, the race will never reach to the finish point.

It is a meaningful and reciprocal process in which individuals who have benefited from mentorship give back by becoming mentors themselves. This act of mentorship not only enriches the lives of mentees but also brings a sense of fulfillment and personal growth to mentors. In this exploration, we'll delve into the importance and benefits of becoming a mentor and the impact it has on both the mentor and the mentee.

One of the primary motivations for individuals to become mentors is the desire to share their knowledge, skills, and experiences with others. Having benefitted from the guidance of their own mentors, they recognize the value of paying it forward. Mentors can provide valuable insights, offer practical advice, and help mentees navigate challenges based on their own journeys.

Mentors often have a deep sense of gratitude for the guidance they received, and they want to give back to their communities or industries. By mentoring others, they contribute to the growth and development of the next generation of professionals, fostering a sense of continuity and legacy in their fields.

Mentorship provides an opportunity for mentors to refine their leadership and coaching abilities. As they guide mentees in setting goals, making decisions, and overcoming challenges, mentors become more effective communicators and leaders. These skills are transferable and valuable in various aspects of life, including the workplace.

Mentors can play a crucial role in promoting diversity and inclusion by mentoring individuals from underrepresented backgrounds. By offering support and guidance to a diverse group of mentees, mentors help create more inclusive and equitable environments in their communities or workplaces.

Becoming a mentor can be personally fulfilling. Witnessing the growth and success of mentees as a result of their guidance and support can be deeply rewarding. This sense of fulfillment stems from knowing that mentors have positively impacted someone's life and contributed to their mentees' achievements.

> ***"Mentors are the lighthouses in the sea of uncertainty, guiding us to the shores of knowledge."***

15

THE DIGITAL DETOX: RECLAIMING YOURTIME AND ATTENTION

In our hyper-connected world, where the digital landscape has woven itself into the very fabric of our daily lives, the notion of a "digital detox" has risen to prominence. It's a concept that has gained traction not only among tech-wary individuals but has also found its place in the ever-evolving lifestyles of celebrities. Indeed, in today's fast-paced, digitally driven society, it has become quite fashionable for the glitterati to take a well-publicized break from their digital platforms—a trend that leaves us pondering: Why would individuals who thrive on digital attention choose to disconnect?

This intriguing paradox shines a spotlight on a deeper issue that resonates with people from all walks of life: the relentless assault of digital overload. The omnipresence of smartphones, the ceaseless allure of social media, and the constant beckoning of notifications have, for many, turned the once-sacred realm of personal time and attention into a battleground. The consequences of this digital invasion are clear: increased stress, pervasive anxiety, and the gradual erosion of genuine human connection.

But the digital detox offers a glimmer of hope—a means of pushing back against the relentless tide of digital saturation. It represents a conscious choice to step away from the screens, to unplug temporarily, and to reclaim our time and attention in a world that often feels overwhelming. This trend, initially popularized by celebrities, has evolved into a vital tool for anyone seeking solace and balance in this digital age.

As we go further, we will embark on a journey through the world of digital detox, exploring its origins, its methods, and its profound benefits. We will delve into the experiences of celebrities who have chosen to disconnect and examine the tangible improvements in their lives. We will also explore the challenges of overcoming digital addiction and the joy of rediscovering the analog world. Ultimately, we will uncover the path to sustaining a balanced digital lifestyle—a lifestyle that allows us to harness the benefits of technology without succumbing to its overwhelming demands.

So, whether you are a celebrity seeking respite from the digital limelight or an everyday individual yearning for a digital sanctuary, this exploration of the digital detox is your guide to reclaiming your time and attention in an increasingly connected world. It's time to embrace the fashion of disconnection, to find balance amid the digital chaos, and to embark on a journey towards a more mindful and fulfilling life.

> ***"Disconnect to reconnect. A digital detox is your passport to rediscover the world beyond the screen."***

THE RISE OF DIGITAL OVERLOAD

Nowadays, it is fashionable for celebrities to take a step back from their digital platforms. The question arises: why would individuals who thrive on digital attention choose to disconnect? The answer lies in the rising tide of digital overload.

In the not-so-distant past, the internet was a novelty, and mobile phones were primarily used for calls and texts. But as technology advanced at an astonishing pace, these devices evolved into multifaceted tools, housing not only our contacts but our calendars, our entertainment, our work, and even our identities. The internet became a vast, interconnected ecosystem where everything was just a click or a swipe away.

The allure of this brave new world was undeniable. We reveled in the convenience of instant communication, the endless information at our fingertips, and the ability to curate and broadcast our lives to an audience that spanned the globe. Social media platforms emerged, transforming the way we interacted with the world and with each other. However, as the digital landscape expanded, so did its demands on our time and attention. Smartphones evolved into pocket-sized supercomputers, capable of delivering a constant stream of news, updates, and notifications. Social media platforms, designed to be addictive, vied for our attention with ever-refreshing feeds and endless scrolling.

The line between work and personal life blurred as emails and messages infiltrated our evenings and weekends.

In the midst of this digital revolution, a profound shift occurred—a shift that would ultimately lead to the rise of digital overload. People began to feel an incessant need to stay connected, to keep up with the relentless flow of information, and to maintain a constant online presence. Fear of missing out became a common affliction, and the pressure to engage in the digital sphere reached unprecedented levels.

This relentless connectivity came at a cost. Studies began to reveal the toll it was taking on our mental health. Anxiety and depression rates climbed, with experts pointing to the excessive use of smartphones and social media as significant contributing factors. The constant exposure to carefully curated online personas led to unrealistic comparisons and a sense of inadequacy. Real-life conversations, once a cornerstone of human interaction, suffered as people stared at screens rather than into each other's eyes.

The erosion of genuine human connection was a particularly poignant consequence of this digital overload. While social media platforms promised to bring people closer together, they often left individuals feeling more isolated and disconnected than ever. The art of face-to-face conversation and deep, meaningful relationships seemed to be slipping through our digital fingertips.

As the digital world expanded exponentially, so did the amount of information we were expected to consume. The 24-hour news cycle bombarded us with headlines, many designed to provoke outrage or fear. The addictive nature of endless scrolling led to information overload, making it increasingly difficult to distinguish between the meaningful and the trivial.

In this era of digital excess, it's no wonder that celebrities, who are constantly in the public eye, began to lead the way in recognizing the need for a break. They understood the profound impact of digital overload on mental well-being and personal relationships. Their choice to temporarily step away from the digital limelight signaled a shift in our collective consciousness—a recognition that the constant barrage of information and connectivity came at a price.

"The real magic happens when you turn off the digital noise and tune into the whispers of your soul."

THE ART OF DIGITAL DETOX

In a world where digital overload has become the new normal, the idea of stepping back from the digital whirlwind and embracing a digital detox might seem like an oasis in a desert of constant connectivity. But what does a digital detox entail, and how can you embark on this journey of self-discovery and reclamation of time and attention?

The first step in mastering the art of digital detox is to recognize the need for it. This may sound straightforward, but in a culture that glorifies constant connectivity and glorifies the always-on lifestyle, admitting that digital overload is affecting your well-being can be challenging. Yet, acknowledging this reality is the cornerstone of your journey toward a healthier relationship with technology.

With that realization in mind, let's explore the practical steps one can take to disconnect from the digital world temporarily and embark on a digital detox:

1. **Setting Boundaries:** The digital detox begins with setting clear boundaries. This involves defining when, where, and how you will engage with digital devices and platforms. It may mean designating specific times for checking emails and social media, turning off notifications outside of work hours, or creating device-free zones in your home.
2. **Creating a Digital Detox Plan:** Like any journey, a digital detox requires planning. Develop a structured plan that outlines the duration of your detox, your goals, and the specific actions you will take. Having a plan in place helps you stay focused and committed to the detox process.
3. **Choosing the Right Time:** Timing is crucial when embarking on a digital detox. Select a period that aligns with your personal and professional commitments. While it might not always be feasible to completely disconnect for an extended period, even short breaks can provide significant benefits.
4. **Notifying Others:** Letting friends, family, and colleagues know about your digital detox can help manage expectations. Informing them about your intentions and the best ways to reach you during your detox can reduce potential misunderstandings and ensure support from your immediate social circle.
5. **Digital Declutter:** Before you begin your detox, take the time to declutter your digital life. Unsubscribe from unnecessary email lists, unfollow accounts that do not

bring value to your life, and delete apps that you seldom use. This will simplify your digital environment and reduce distractions.

6. **Alternative Activities:** Identify activities that you can engage in during your digital detox. Consider reading physical books, spending time in nature, practicing mindfulness, or pursuing a hobby that has taken a back seat to your digital life. These activities will help fill the void left by digital disconnection.
7. **Digital Sabbatical:** To fully immerse yourself in the detox experience, consider a digital sabbatical. This involves a complete break from all digital devices for a specified period. During this time, you'll discover a sense of liberation from the constant demands of the digital world.
8. **Journaling:** Keeping a journal throughout your digital detox can be incredibly insightful. Document your thoughts, feelings, and experiences during this period. Reflecting on your journey can help you gain a deeper understanding of your digital habits and their impact on your life.
9. **Practice Mindfulness:** Mindfulness techniques can be invaluable during a digital detox. Learn to be fully present in the moment, whether you're taking a walk, enjoying a meal, or engaging in a conversation. Mindfulness can help you appreciate life's simple pleasures without digital distractions.
10. **Seek Support:** Remember that you don't have to embark on a digital detox journey alone. Share your goals with friends or join online communities dedicated to digital detoxing. Engaging with others who are also striving for a

healthier digital balance can provide encouragement and motivation.

In the quest to master the art of digital detox, these practical steps serve as your compass. As you navigate this journey, you will discover that it's not about rejecting technology but rather about regaining control over your relationship with it. In the following chapters, we will delve deeper into the benefits of disconnecting, drawing inspiration from celebrities and individuals who have successfully embraced the digital detox lifestyle.

THE BENEFITS OF DISCONNECTING

In the age of constant connectivity, where digital devices accompany us from the moment we wake up to the instant before we drift into slumber, the notion of voluntarily disconnecting from this digital umbilical cord might seem counterintuitive. Yet, as celebrities and an increasing number of individuals have discovered, there is a treasure trove of benefits waiting to be unearthed when we take the courageous step of embarking on a digital detox.

The allure of the digital world is undeniable. The instant gratification of social media likes, the endless stream of news and entertainment, and the promise of constant connection with friends and acquaintances have woven a compelling web. However, beneath this shimmering surface lie the hidden costs of digital overload.

THE MENTAL HEALTH RENAISSANCE

One of the most profound benefits of a digital detox is the restoration of mental health. The constant exposure to carefully curated digital personas, the anxiety-inducing effects of notifications, and the incessant pressure to keep up with the digital Joneses have taken a toll on our psychological well-being.

Reduced Stress and Anxiety: Disconnecting from the digital world provides an immediate respite from the constant stressors that often accompany it. Studies have shown that even a short break from social media can lead to a significant reduction in stress and anxiety levels. The ceaseless comparison to others, the fear of missing out, and the relentless quest for validation through likes and comments gradually lose their grip.

Improved Sleep: The glowing screens of our devices emit blue light, which interferes with the production of melatonin, the hormone responsible for regulating sleep. As a result, many of us find it challenging to achieve restful sleep when we're constantly exposed to screens. A digital detox allows for better sleep patterns, leading to improved overall well-being.

Enhanced Focus and Productivity: The constant interruptions caused by notifications and the lure of digital distractions can hinder productivity and focus. Disconnecting provides an opportunity to regain your ability to concentrate on tasks without the constant pull of your digital devices.

Increased Self-Awareness: The introspective nature of a digital detox encourages self-reflection. As you disconnect from external digital stimuli, you have the chance to reconnect with your inner thoughts, desires, and aspirations. This newfound self-awareness can be transformative and lead to personal growth.

REDISCOVERING AUTHENTIC CONNECTIONS

While the digital world promises connection, it often delivers a shallow facsimile of genuine human interaction. A digital detox can be a catalyst for rediscovering the richness of authentic connections.

Deeper Relationships: Stepping away from screens allows for more meaningful face-to-face interactions with friends and loved ones. It provides the space and time to nurture deeper relationships, fostering empathy, understanding, and a sense of belonging.

Mindful Communication: In a world of instant messaging and emoji-driven conversations, the art of mindful and empathetic communication can atrophy. A digital detox encourages a return to meaningful conversations where words carry weight, and genuine emotions are expressed.

Reconnecting with Nature: Many who embark on a digital detox find themselves reconnecting with the natural world. Whether it's taking a leisurely walk in the park or going on a hiking adventure, the absence of digital distractions allows for a deeper appreciation of the beauty and serenity of the outdoors.

THE RETURN TO PRODUCTIVE LIVING

One of the most tangible benefits of a digital detox is the reclamation of time and productivity.

Increased Leisure Time: Without the constant tug of digital distractions, individuals often discover newfound leisure time. This can be spent pursuing hobbies, reading, engaging in physical activities, or simply enjoying moments of stillness.

Boosted Creativity: A digital detox can reignite your creativity. Freed from the constraints of endless scrolling and content consumption, you may find inspiration in unexpected places and have the mental space to create, innovate, and explore new ideas.

Balanced Work-Life Integration: For those who use digital devices for work, a digital detox can be a vital tool for achieving a healthy work-life balance. It allows you to set clear boundaries and maintain a separation between professional responsibilities and personal time.

As we explore the benefits of disconnecting, it becomes evident that a digital detox is not a retreat from progress but a reevaluation of our relationship with technology. It's a deliberate step toward regaining control over our time, our attention, and our mental well-being in an increasingly connected world. The experiences of celebrities who have embraced this lifestyle provide compelling evidence of the transformative power of a digital detox, serving as a source of inspiration for individuals seeking to unlock its myriad benefits. In the following chapters, we will delve deeper into the practicalities of overcoming digital addiction and maintaining a balanced digital lifestyle.

> ***"A digital detox is the pause button for your soul, allowing you to replay life's most meaningful moments."***

OVERCOMING DIGITAL ADDICTION

The term "addiction" has long been associated with substances like drugs and alcohol, but in the digital age, a new type of addiction has emerged—one that doesn't involve chemical substances but is just as potent and pervasive: digital addiction. As celebrities have demonstrated, conquering this addiction can be a challenging yet profoundly liberating experience. In this chapter, we will delve into the depths of digital addiction, understanding its roots and offering practical strategies to break free from its grasp.

Digital addiction is a multifaceted phenomenon characterized by compulsive and excessive use of digital devices and platforms. It can manifest in various forms, including:

1. **Social Media Addiction:** This type of addiction revolves around the constant need to check and engage with social media platforms. Individuals addicted to social media may experience anxiety or discomfort when they are unable to access their accounts regularly.
2. **Smartphone Addiction:** Smartphone addiction involves an almost pathological attachment to one's phone, often resulting in incessant checking, even in inappropriate or dangerous situations. It can lead to physical symptoms

such as "phantom vibrations," where individuals perceive notifications that aren't actually there.

3. **Internet Addiction:** Internet addiction encompasses a wide range of compulsive online behaviors, from excessive gaming and gambling to obsessive internet browsing. It can significantly interfere with daily life and responsibilities.
4. **Email Addiction:** Some individuals develop an addiction to checking and responding to emails, even outside of work hours. This addiction can lead to heightened stress levels and disrupt work-life balance.

> ***"Detox your digital life, and you'll discover the art of being fully alive."***

One of the first steps in overcoming digital addiction is identifying the triggers that drive compulsive digital behavior. Common triggers include:

1. **Boredom:** Many people turn to their digital devices when they are bored, using them as a source of entertainment and distraction. Recognizing this pattern and finding alternative ways to combat boredom is crucial.
2. **Stress and Anxiety:** Digital devices can provide a temporary escape from stress and anxiety. Unfortunately, excessive digital use often exacerbates these feelings in the long run. Learning healthy coping mechanisms for stress is essential.
3. **Fear of Missing Out:** The fear of missing out on social events, news, or updates can drive compulsive digital behavior. It's important to recognize that most information will still be available when you choose to access it.

4. **Social Pressure:** Peer pressure and societal expectations can also contribute to digital addiction. The feeling of needing to keep up with friends or colleagues can be powerful, but it's essential to prioritize your well-being.

> ***"In the world of constant connectivity, a digital detox is your sanctuary of serenity."***

Breaking free from digital addiction requires commitment and effort, but the rewards are immeasurable. Here are practical strategies to help you on your journey to recovery:

1. **Digital Detox Challenge:** Start with a short digital detox challenge. Set aside a specific period, such as a weekend, during which you will disconnect from your digital devices. Use this time to assess the impact of digital addiction on your life.
2. **Digital Usage Tracking:** Keep a journal of your digital usage. Record the amount of time you spend on various devices and platforms each day. This self-awareness can help you identify patterns and areas where you need to cut back.
3. **Delete Unnecessary Apps:** Remove apps and digital distractions that contribute to your addiction. Simplify your digital environment to reduce temptation.
4. **Set Screen Time Limits:** Most smartphones offer screen time management features that allow you to set daily limits for specific apps or activities. Utilize these tools to regain control over your digital usage.
5. **Create Technology-Free Zones:** Designate certain areas of your home or specific times of day as technology-free zones. For example, establish a no-phone rule during meals or in the bedroom.

6. **Seek Professional Help:** If you find that your digital addiction is significantly impacting your life and well-being, consider seeking professional help from therapists or support groups that specialize in digital addiction.
7. **Engage in Offline Activities:** Fill the void left by digital addiction with offline activities that you enjoy. Pursue hobbies, exercise, read books, or spend quality time with loved ones.
8. **Practice Mindfulness:** Mindfulness techniques can help you become more aware of your digital impulses and cravings. Mindfulness can empower you to make conscious choices about when and how you engage with technology.
9. **Build a Support Network:** Share your journey with friends or family members who can provide encouragement and accountability. Connecting with others who are also overcoming digital addiction can be particularly beneficial.

Breaking free from digital addiction is not a onetime event but a gradual process that requires patience and persistence. It involves rewiring your habits and cultivating a healthier relationship with technology. As you embark on this journey, remember that you are not alone; countless individuals, including celebrities, have successfully conquered their digital dependencies, leading to improved mental health, enhanced productivity, and a greater sense of fulfillment. In the subsequent chapters, we will explore the art of reconnecting with the analog world and sustaining a balanced digital lifestyle.

> ***"Your worth is not determined by your online presence. A digital detox reminds you of the authenticity you bring to the world."***

RECONNECTING WITH THE ANALOG WORLD

In our modern, digitally driven lives, the concept of reconnecting with the analog world might seem like a journey to a distant past, a place where life unfolded at a slower pace, and human connections were deeper and more meaningful. Yet, it is precisely this reconnection that forms a pivotal part of the digital detox experience, offering a chance to rediscover the simple joys of life and a profound sense of presence.

As you embark on your digital detox journey, the initial phase of disconnecting from the digital world can be both liberating and disorienting. Suddenly, the constant stream of notifications, the relentless scroll of social media, and the digital distractions that once filled your days begin to fade into the background.

In this quietude, you may find yourself grappling with moments of unease, a restless sense of missing out, or an uncertainty about how to occupy your time. It is precisely at this juncture that the analog world beckons—a world brimming with opportunities for rediscovery and rejuvenation.

One of the most delightful aspects of disconnecting from the digital world is the opportunity to rediscover the timeless pleasure of reading physical books. In the digital age, many of us have transitioned to e-books, audiobooks, or digital articles, often missing the tangible connection that comes from holding a book in our hands.

As you delve into the pages of a physical book, you may find that the act of turning each page becomes a meditative ritual. The smell of ink and paper, the texture of the pages beneath your fingers, and the immersive experience of losing yourself in a well-crafted narrative—all of these elements combine to create a multisensory delight that digital reading cannot replicate.

The digital age has transformed the way we communicate, emphasizing speed and brevity at the expense of depth and nuance.

While digital communication has its merits, there is no substitute for the richness of face-to-face conversations.

As you embark on your digital detox, you may find yourself reconnecting with friends, family members, and colleagues in ways that transcend the limitations of text messages and emojis. In-person conversations allow for the exchange of subtle facial expressions, tone of voice, and body language—all of which contribute to a deeper understanding of one another.

In the digital world, our attention is often fixated on screens, and we may find ourselves oblivious to the natural world that surrounds us. A digital detox provides an opportunity to rekindle our connection with nature.

Whether you take leisurely strolls in the park, go for long hikes in the wilderness, or simply spend time in your garden, nature offers solace, beauty, and a sense of serenity that can be profoundly restorative. Disconnecting from the digital world allows you to appreciate the changing seasons, the rustle of leaves, and the chirping of birds — simple pleasures that may have been overlooked in the digital frenzy.

One of the most valuable gifts of a digital detox is the cultivation of mindfulness—the practice of being fully present in the moment. Mindfulness encourages you to pay attention to your thoughts, emotions, and surroundings without judgment.

As you disconnect from digital distractions, you may discover the beauty of mindfulness in everyday activities. Whether it's savoring a cup of tea, relishing a meal, or watching the sunset, mindfulness can enhance your ability to find joy in the ordinary and the extraordinary moments of life.

The digital world often competes for our attention, leaving little room for analog hobbies and creative pursuits. However, a digital detox creates the space for you to revisit or discover new hobbies that exist beyond the screen.

Whether you immerse yourself in painting, crafting, playing a musical instrument, gardening, or cooking, these analog activities provide a sense of accomplishment, creativity, and fulfillment that digital experiences cannot replicate.

In the midst of digital overload, it's easy to lose sight of who we truly are and what truly matters to us. The digital detox journey allows you to peel away the layers of digital distraction and rediscover your authentic self.

As you spend more time engaged in analog activities and meaningful connections, you may gain insights into your passions, values, and goals. This self-discovery can be a profound and transformative aspect of the digital detox experience.

The art of reconnecting with the analog world is not about rejecting technology but rather about achieving a harmonious balance between the digital and the analog. The insights gained during a digital detox can inform the way you engage with technology in the future.

As you navigate the landscape of analog experiences, you will find that your relationship with the digital world becomes more intentional. You may establish boundaries that allow you to enjoy the benefits of technology without succumbing to its overwhelming demands. The result is a balanced digital lifestyle—one that enhances your well-being, deepens your connections, and enriches your life in ways you never imagined.

> ***"In the quiet of a digital detox, you'll hear the stories your heart has been longing to tell."***

SUSTAINING A BALANCED DIGITAL LIFESTYLE

As your digital detox journey progresses, you've likely experienced the transformative power of disconnecting from the digital world and reconnecting with the analog. This chapter explores the critical phase of sustaining a balanced digital lifestyle—a phase that transcends the initial detox period and aims to integrate the lessons learned into your everyday life. Achieving this balance involves maintaining a healthy relationship with technology, practicing digital mindfulness, and setting long-term boundaries.

Digital mindfulness is a practice that encourages you to engage with technology deliberately, consciously, and in ways that align with your values and well-being. It involves the following key principles:

1. **Intentional Technology Use:** Before picking up your device or logging onto a platform, ask yourself why you're doing it. Is it to connect with friends, learn something new, or relax? Being intentional about your digital activities helps you avoid mindless scrolling and prioritize activities that truly matter to you.
2. **Mindful Consumption:** When you consume digital content, be aware of its impact on your thoughts and emotions. Consider whether the content is uplifting or draining. Cultivate the habit of curating your digital environment to include sources of inspiration and positivity.
3. **Digital Sabbaticals:** Periodic digital sabbaticals, even if shorter than your initial detox, can help you reset and recharge. Designate specific days or times when you disconnect entirely, allowing your mind to rest and rejuvenate.
4. **Limit Multitasking:** Multitasking between digital devices and tasks can diminish your focus and productivity. Practice unitasking—devoting your full attention to one task at a time—whether it's work, reading, or engaging with loved ones.

5. **Mindful Notifications:** Reevaluate your notification settings to reduce distractions. Disable non-essential notifications and opt for a "notification-free" period during focused work or personal time.
6. **Regular Self-Reflection:** Dedicate time for self- reflection to assess your digital habits and their impact on your life. This ongoing practice helps you stay attuned to your relationship with technology and make necessary adjustments.

It is crucial for sustaining a balanced digital lifestyle. These boundaries protect your personal time, relationships, and overall well-being. Consider the following strategies:

1. **Define Digital-Free Zones:** Designate specific areas in your home where digital devices are not allowed. For example, keep your bedroom and dining area free of screens to promote better sleep and quality family time.
2. **Create Screen-Free Times:** Set aside dedicated periods during the day when screens are off-limits. This may include the first hour after waking up, mealtimes, or the last hour before bedtime.
3. **Family Digital Agreements:** Engage your family members in discussions about healthy digital use. Collaboratively establish rules and boundaries that work for everyone, ensuring quality family time and open communication.
4. **Work-Life Balance:** If your profession involves digital devices, establish clear boundaries between work and personal life. Designate specific hours for work-related tasks and disconnect during non-work hours to maintain balance.
5. **Digital-Free Activities:** Make a list of activities you enjoy that do not involve digital devices. Engage in these

activities regularly to balance your digital consumption with real-world experiences.

6. **Prioritize Face-to-Face Interaction:** Cultivate in- person relationships by scheduling regular face-to-face meetups with friends and loved ones. Foster deeper connections through meaningful conversations and shared experiences.
7. **Regular Digital Detox Retreats:** Plan periodic digital detox retreats, even if they are shorter than your initial detox. These retreats serve as checkpoints for recalibrating your digital habits.

Sustaining a balanced digital lifestyle is not about rejecting technology; rather, it's about embracing it consciously and in moderation. As you continue on this journey, you'll reap numerous benefits:

1. **Enhanced Productivity:** By practicing digital mindfulness and setting boundaries, you'll experience improved focus and productivity in both your personal and professional life.
2. **Better Mental Health:** A balanced digital lifestyle reduces digital overload, which, in turn, contributes to reduced stress and anxiety. You'll have greater mental clarity and emotional well-being.
3. **Deeper Relationships:** Nurturing face-to-face connections and meaningful conversations strengthens your relationships and fosters a sense of belonging.
4. **Increased Creativity:** Disconnecting from the digital world allows your mind to wander and explore creative ideas. You'll find renewed inspiration and innovation.
5. **Heightened Awareness:** Mindful living cultivates a heightened awareness of the present moment, enabling

you to appreciate life's simple pleasures and engage more fully in your experiences.

6. **Greater Control:** By actively managing your digital habits, you regain control over your time and attention. You'll no longer be a passive consumer of digital content but an intentional participant in your digital life.
7. **Improved Sleep:** A balanced digital lifestyle supports healthy sleep patterns, resulting in better rest and overall health.

As you continue to practice digital mindfulness and maintain boundaries with technology, remember that sustaining a balanced digital lifestyle is an ongoing journey. It requires adaptability, self-awareness, and a commitment to prioritizing your well-being in a digital world. The experiences of celebrities who have successfully embraced this lifestyle serve as a testament to the enduring rewards of a mindful and balanced relationship with technology. In concluding this exploration of the digital detox, you are equipped with the knowledge and tools to navigate the digital age with intention, purpose, and a profound sense of fulfillment.

"Pause. Breathe. Disconnect. A digital detox is the ultimate 'self-care' for your soul."

16

EXPLORING SPIRITUALITY: CONNECTING WITH THE DIVINE FOR INNER FULFILLMENT

India, a timeless realm steeped in history and mysticism, has earned its epithet as "the land of spiritual diversity" through a remarkable confluence of cultures, traditions, and philosophical ideologies. Across its vast expanse, from the snow-capped Himalayas to the sun-kissed shores of its peninsular borders, spirituality pulsates through the veins of its people, shaping their beliefs, values, and way of life. This ancient nation boasts a spiritual tapestry adorned with intricate patterns, woven by the interplay of rituals, customs, and a profound connection to the ethereal.

In this intricate tapestry, a multitude of gods and goddesses are revered, each an embodiment of virtues and cosmic forces. From the benevolent Ganesh to the fierce Durga, from the compassionate Buddha to the yogic Shiva, each entity beckons devotees to a unique path, while collectively leading towards the ultimate goal: mental peace and inner fulfillment.

Within the intricate blend of beliefs, practices, and rituals, we aspire to uncover the perennial pursuit of profound tranquility that binds the souls of this ancient land. Join us as we traverse the spiritual terrain of India, delving deeper into the facets that echo the collective heartbeat of a nation in pursuit of the divine within and without.

THE MULTITUDE OF DEITIES: A TAPESTRY OF DIVINE REPRESENTATIONS

In the vast and intricate spiritual landscape of India, the multitude of deities stands as a testament to the depth and richness of its spiritual heritage. These revered figures are not mere idols but symbolic representations of the profound philosophies and values that guide the lives of the devout.

A. PHILOSOPHICAL INTERPRETATIONS

India's pantheon of deities stems from ancient philosophical underpinnings. For instance, Brahma, Vishnu, and Shiva, the Hindu Trinity, embody the cosmic processes of creation, preservation, and destruction respectively, symbolizing the cyclical nature of existence. Lakshmi, the goddess of wealth and prosperity, epitomizes abundance and auspiciousness, reflecting the importance of prosperity in the lives of people. These philosophical interpretations provide a moral compass and offer solace in the face of life's challenges.

B. REGIONAL AND CULTURAL VARIANCES

One of the remarkable aspects of India's spiritual tapestry is the regional and cultural variations in deity worship. Each region might have its own set of deities, revered due to local beliefs, historical events, or cultural influences. For instance, the southern state of Tamil Nadu venerates Murugan, the warrior god, while the northern state of Rajasthan holds a special reverence for Karni Mata, the goddess of rats. These variations enrich the spiritual fabric of the nation, promoting tolerance, acceptance, and a celebration of diversity.

C. STORIES AND EPICS

The pantheon of deities is interwoven with captivating stories and epic narratives found in ancient scriptures like the Vedas,

Upanishads, Ramayana, Mahabharata, and Puranas. These narratives elucidate the divine attributes, virtues, and heroic feats of the deities. For example, the tale of Lord Rama in the Ramayana exemplifies righteousness, courage, and devotion, providing a moral compass for devotees.

D. PERSONAL DEVOTION AND CONNECTION

Individuals often resonate with specific deities based on their personal inclinations, aspirations, and life circumstances. Devotees form a deep, personal connection with a chosen deity, believing that the chosen deity bestows blessings and guidance aligned with their desires and challenges. This personal devotion cultivates a sense of closeness and emotional solace, promoting a profound bond with the divine.

E. RITUALS AND OFFERINGS

Worshiping deities involves a plethora of rituals, ceremonies, and offerings that vary based on the deity and the traditions of a particular community or family. These rituals range from simple daily prayers to elaborate festivals and ceremonies. Offerings like flowers, incense, fruits, and sweets symbolize devotion, purity, and gratitude, enhancing the spiritual connection with the divine.

HOW TO EMBARK ON THE PATH TO THE DIVINE?

Embarking on the path to the divine is a profound and personal journey, necessitating a genuine desire for spiritual awakening and a deeper connection with the transcendent. It is a voyage into the depths of your being, seeking to uncover the essence of life and existence. One of the fundamental steps on this path is self-reflection and self-inquiry. Begin by understanding your spiritual aspirations. What is it that you seek in your spiritual journey? Is it inner peace, purpose, meaning, or a sense of connection with something beyond the material world?

In this exploration of self, examining your existing beliefs and values is crucial. Take time to introspect and question whether your current beliefs align with the spiritual path you intend to traverse. This introspection is not about abandoning beliefs, but about ensuring that your chosen path resonates with your core values and beliefs, forming a solid foundation for your spiritual journey.

Education and knowledge are the next steps on this voyage. Immerse yourself in the study of spiritual traditions, philosophies, and practices. Understanding diverse spiritual traditions broadens your perspective and equips you with the knowledge to choose a path that aligns with your heart and mind.

Exploring philosophical concepts related to the divine, consciousness, existence, and the nature of reality is equally important. Philosophy offers a deeper comprehension of abstract concepts, providing a mental framework for your spiritual journey. Through philosophical exploration, you can contemplate the profound questions of life, leading to a more profound understanding of the spiritual path you wish to follow.

Meditation and mindfulness constitute pillars of spiritual practice. Establishing a regular meditation practice forms the heart of this journey. Begin with short, focused sessions and gradually increase the duration as you become more comfortable. Meditation quietens the mind, enhances self-awareness, and facilitates a deeper connection with the divine within and beyond. Extend mindfulness beyond the confines of your meditation practice, incorporating it into your daily life. Cultivate the ability to be present in every moment, whether you are eating, walking, or engaging with others. This mindful living amplifies your spiritual awareness and brings you closer to the divine essence that permeates all aspects of existence.

Embarking on the path to the divine is a transformative journey. It is a journey of self-discovery, a pilgrimage within, where you seek to unravel the mysteries of existence and attain a state of inner peace and spiritual awakening. Each step along this path brings you closer to your true self, and as you immerse yourself in the depths of spirituality, you will discover a profound connection with the divine and an everlasting sense of fulfillment and purpose.

YOGA AND MEDITATION IN INDIA: GATEWAYS TO THE DIVINE PATH

Yoga, derived from the Sanskrit word "yuj", meaning union, embodies the holistic integration of the physical, mental, and spiritual dimensions of human existence. Its purpose is to unite the individual consciousness with the universal consciousness. Through a variety of practices, including physical postures (asanas), breath control (pranayama), ethical principles (yamas and niyamas), concentration (dharana), and meditation (dhyana), yoga seeks to achieve a harmonious balance between the body, mind, and soul.

The ultimate goal of yoga, as outlined in Patanjali's Yoga Sutras, is Samadhi—a state of deep meditation and spiritual absorption where the practitioner experiences oneness with the divine.

Meditation, an integral component of yoga, is the art of training the mind to achieve a state of heightened awareness and inner tranquility.

Meditation techniques vary—from focused attention on the breath (anapanasati) to mindfulness meditation, loving-kindness meditation (metta), and transcendental meditation. Regardless of the method, the objective remains the same: to quiet the mind, cultivate self-awareness, and experience the true nature of reality beyond the confines of the ego.

The value of yoga and meditation in the spiritual journey lies in their capacity to provide seekers with the necessary tools to navigate the complexities of the mind and body.

In the heartland of yoga and meditation, the spiritual seeker is guided to move beyond the physical realm, transcend the fluctuations of the mind, and touch the sublime. By diligently practicing these ancient arts, individuals can unlock the door to the divine, realizing that their essence is an inseparable part of the universal consciousness, leading them to a life of purpose, bliss, and a deeper understanding of the interconnectedness of all creation.

THE PATH OF DIVINE: UNVEILING KARMA AND DHARMA BEYOND RITUALS

A prevalent misconception exists regarding the path of the divine, often equating it with ritualistic worship and religious chores. However, at its core, the path to the divine transcends mere ceremonies; it is intricately tied to the principles of karma and dharma. Understanding this essence requires a deeper exploration of these fundamental concepts deeply embedded in Indian philosophy.

1. KARMA: ACTIONS AND CONSEQUENCES

Karma, often reduced to a simplified 'action equals reaction' formula, encompasses a much broader and profound concept. It is the law of cause and effect, implying that every action, whether physical, mental, or emotional, has consequences. These consequences shape an individual's future experiences, circumstances, and ultimately their destiny.

In the context of the path to the divine, karma emphasizes conscious and intentional actions aligned with dharma—actions driven by righteousness, duty, and ethical conduct. It encourages individuals to act in harmony with the universe, promoting empathy, compassion, and positive contributions to the world.

2. DHARMA: THE RIGHTEOUS PATH

Dharma, often translated as "duty" or "righteousness", is a multifaceted concept deeply ingrained in Indian philosophy. It is the moral and ethical path, the set of responsibilities and duties that one must follow based on their position in society, age, gender, and other factors. Dharma guides an individual to live a life of righteousness, balancing personal desires with the needs of society and the universe.

In the context of the divine path, dharma encourages individuals to fulfill their duties and responsibilities with utmost sincerity, aligning actions with moral principles. This involves upholding truth, showing compassion, respecting others, and acting for the greater good, thereby attaining spiritual growth and self-realization.

3. BEYOND RITUALS: EMBRACING THE ESSENCE

The misunderstanding often arises from a focus on rituals and ceremonies, perceiving them as the primary means to attain divine connection. While rituals have their place in various spiritual practices, they are not the ultimate goal but a means to reinforce the understanding of karma and dharma. Rituals, when performed with the right intent and understanding, can instill a sense of discipline, devotion, and spiritual consciousness.

However, true spiritual growth occurs when individuals move beyond the superficiality of rituals and wholeheartedly embrace the principles of karma and dharma in their daily lives. It involves conscious decision-making, ethical conduct, and an unwavering commitment to one's responsibilities and duties in every sphere of life.

SEVA: THE ULTIMATE PATH OF THE DIVINE

Seva, the selfless act of service or altruism, indeed stands as a pinnacle on the path to the divine in many spiritual traditions. Rooted in compassion, empathy, and the desire to alleviate the suffering of others, seva transcends the self and embodies the essence of interconnectedness and oneness.

Seva goes beyond the act of helping; it embodies the intent to serve without expecting anything in return. It is an offering of one's time, skills, and resources to benefit others and the greater good. Seva is an expression of love, kindness, and empathy, reflecting the interconnectedness of all beings.

In Indian philosophy, seva finds its foundation in the principles of karma and dharma. It's a way to practice righteous action (dharma) and positive karma. By selflessly serving others, individuals align their actions with the natural flow of the universe and contribute to its harmony. The Bhagavad Gita, a revered text in Hindu philosophy, emphasizes the importance of performing one's duty (dharma) and selfless service. Lord Krishna instructs Arjuna about righteous action and the significance of fulfilling one's responsibilities without attachment to outcomes.

Throughout Indian mythology and history, stories of saints and sages highlight their life of service and compassion. Figures like Swami Vivekananda, Mother Teresa, and Mahatma Gandhi devoted their lives to serving humanity, showcasing that seva is a path to divine realization.

Seva helps individuals recognize the interconnectedness of all life. Through service, they understand that serving others is akin to serving the divine, as the divine exists in every being.

Volunteering for community-based organizations, contributing to local projects, or participating in initiatives for social welfare and development are forms of seva.

Providing assistance to the less fortunate, whether through donating food, clothing, or offering your skills for their benefit, is a form of seva.

Engaging in educational initiatives, tutoring, or sponsoring education for underprivileged children are impactful ways to serve society.

In summary, seva is not only a selfless act but a spiritual path that leads to the divine. By dedicating oneself to the service of others and embodying love and compassion, individuals elevate their consciousness, transcend selfishness, and ultimately realize their interconnectedness with all creation. In the tapestry of spirituality, seva is the golden thread that weaves together the fabric of selflessness, humility, and divine love.

17

EMBRACING IMPERFECTION: THE BEAUTY IN BEING HUMAN

In a world inundated with images of flawlessness and ideals of perfection, the concept of embracing imperfection may seem counterintuitive, even radical. Yet, within the very fabric of our existence lies a profound truth: it is our imperfections that make us beautifully human. In this exploration, we delve into the depths of what it truly means to embrace imperfection and discover the inherent beauty that resides within our flaws.

To embrace imperfection is not to resign ourselves to mediocrity or stagnation; rather, it is to embrace the full spectrum of our humanity—the messy, imperfect, beautifully flawed essence of who we are. It is a recognition that perfection is not only unattainable but also undesirable, for it is in our imperfections that we find our truest selves.

In the pursuit of perfection, we often find ourselves trapped in a relentless cycle of comparison and self-criticism, constantly measuring our worth against unattainable standards set by society or ourselves. Yet, this pursuit only serves to breed discontent and self-doubt, obscuring the inherent beauty that lies within our imperfections.

Embracing imperfection requires a shift in perspective—a reevaluation of our understanding of what it means to be human. It is an invitation to embrace vulnerability, to acknowledge our flaws and limitations, and to find strength and resilience in the face of adversity.

It is a journey of self-discovery and self-acceptance, a process of learning to love ourselves—not in spite of our imperfections, but because of them.

In a world that often seeks to erase our imperfections and homogenize our identities, embracing imperfection becomes an act of rebellion—a radical affirmation of our humanity in all its messy, imperfect glory. It is a testament to the resilience of the human spirit, the capacity for growth and transformation, and the enduring power of love and connection.

As we embark on this journey of exploration and discovery, may we find solace in the imperfections that unite us, courage in the vulnerabilities that make us human, and beauty in the flawed, imperfect, exquisitely unique essence of who we are. For it is in embracing our imperfections that we truly discover the beauty in being human.

> ***"Life's canvas is painted not with flawless brush-strokes, but with the bold strokes of imperfection, each stroke adding depth, character, and beauty to the masterpiece of our humanity."***

We all remember the iconic film "Forrest Gump". In the film, we follow the extraordinary life journey of the titular character, Forrest Gump, who is portrayed by Tom Hanks.

One of the most poignant examples of embracing imperfection in the film is Forrest's relationship with Jenny, his childhood friend and love interest. Jenny struggles with her own imperfections and inner demons, grappling with issues such as abuse, addiction, and self-destructive behavior. Despite the complexities of their relationship, Forrest unconditionally accepts Jenny for who she is, flaws and all. He loves her fiercely, offering her unwavering support and understanding throughout her tumultuous journey.

Forrest's friendship with Bubba, his fellow soldier and shrimp enthusiast, is another powerful example of embracing imperfection. Bubba comes from a humble background, and he dreams of starting a shrimp business after the war. Tragically, Bubba's life is cut short during combat, but Forrest honors his friend's memory by fulfilling their shared dream and establishing the Bubba Gump Shrimp Company. In doing so, Forrest embraces imperfection by turning tragedy into triumph, finding beauty and purpose in honoring his friend's legacy.

In essence, "Forrest Gump" serves as a poignant reminder that life is a messy, imperfect journey, filled with highs and lows, triumphs and failures. Yet, it is precisely in embracing our imperfections and accepting the imperfections of others that we discover the true beauty of being human. Just as Forrest Gump navigates life with courage, kindness, and authenticity, so too can we find strength and resilience in embracing our flaws and celebrating the imperfect, yet extraordinary, essence of who we are.

ACKNOWLEDGE, CULTIVATE SELF COMPASSION, EMBRACE AND THEN FIND STRENGTH.

In the journey of embracing imperfection, we encounter a myriad of experiences that shape our understanding of what it means to be human. This chapter serves as a comprehensive exploration of key aspects of embracing imperfection: acknowledging our flaws, cultivating self-compassion, embracing vulnerability, and finding strength in adversity. Together, these elements form the foundation upon which we build a deeper connection with ourselves and others, ultimately leading to a more authentic and fulfilling life.

Acknowledging Our Flaws: By recognizing and owning our flaws, we open ourselves up to growth, self-discovery, and personal transformation. Through anecdotes, reflections, and practical exercises, we explore strategies for embracing our flaws with grace and compassion, fostering a greater sense of authenticity and self-acceptance.

Cultivating Self-Compassion: Central to the journey of embracing imperfection is the practice of self-compassion. Cultivating self-compassion enables us to navigate the challenges of life with greater resilience and kindness towards ourselves. Through guided meditations, journal prompts, and real-life examples, we learn to embrace imperfection with gentleness and understanding, fostering a deeper sense of self-love and acceptance.

Embracing Vulnerability: Vulnerability is often viewed as a weakness, yet it is through our vulnerability that we cultivate authentic connections and meaningful relationships. Vulnerability is a gateway to intimacy, empathy, and genuine human connection.

Finding Strength in Adversity: Life is filled with challenges and setbacks, yet it is often in the face of adversity that we discover our greatest strengths. By reframing our perception of failure and hardship, we can uncover the hidden opportunities for growth, wisdom, and personal empowerment that lie within life's most challenging moments.

> ***"Amidst the chaos of existence, it is in our imperfections that we find our truest selves, for it is through our flaws that the light of our humanity shines brightest."***

18

EMBRACING CHANGE: THRIVING IN TIMES OF TRANSITION

In the ever-evolving life, change is the only constant. From the shifting tides of personal growth to the seismic shifts of societal transformation, the journey of existence is marked by periods of transition and upheaval. Yet, amidst the uncertainty and flux, there exists a profound opportunity—to not merely adapt to change, but to embrace it as a catalyst for growth, resilience, and renewal. In this exploration, we embark on a journey into the heart of change, delving into the depths of what it means to embrace change and thrive amidst transition. From the intricacies of personal transformation to the complexities of navigating societal shifts, we uncover the timeless wisdom and practical insights that empower us to embrace change as a source of strength, creativity, and possibility. "Embracing Change: Thriving in Times of Transition" is not merely a Mantra for survival in an ever-changing world; it is a manifesto for living fully and authentically in the face of uncertainty. It is a testament to the resilience of the human spirit, the capacity for growth and adaptation, and the enduring power of hope and optimism.

From psychology and neuroscience to philosophy and spirituality, we uncover the universal truths and timeless principles that guide us through the tumultuous waters of change.

Through personal anecdotes, practical strategies, and philosophical reflections, we learn to navigate the ebbs and flows of change with grace, courage, and resilience. We discover how to embrace the inherent beauty and possibility of transition, transforming adversity into opportunity and uncertainty into growth.

As we embark on this journey of embracing change, may we find solace in the knowledge that change is not something to be feared or resisted, but embraced as an integral part of the human experience. May we cultivate the courage to step into the unknown, the resilience to weather life's storms, and the wisdom to embrace change as a pathway to greater authenticity, connection, and fulfillment.

For it is in embracing change that we discover the boundless potential of the human spirit—to adapt, evolve, and thrive in times of transition, and to forge a path towards a more resilient, vibrant, and flourishing future.

> ***"Like a phoenix rising from the ashes, we find our strength not in avoiding change, but in embracing it. In the fires of transformation, we are reborn, resilient and unyielding."***

Consider the process of metamorphosis in the life cycle of a butterfly as an example from science to explain embracing change and thriving in times of transition.

Metamorphosis is a profound transformation that occurs in the life of a butterfly, symbolizing the journey of change and transition. The butterfly begins its life as a humble caterpillar, confined to crawling on the ground and consuming leaves for sustenance. However, as it grows and matures, the caterpillar undergoes a remarkable metamorphosis, encapsulated in the chrysalis, a protective shell that shelters it during its transformation.

During this period of transition, the caterpillar undergoes profound changes at a cellular level, breaking down its old body and restructuring itself into a completely new form. It emerges from the chrysalis as a beautiful butterfly, with delicate wings that enable it to soar through the skies, liberated from the constraints of its former existence.

This process of metamorphosis serves as a powerful metaphor for embracing change and thriving in times of transition. Like the caterpillar, we too encounter periods of profound transformation in our lives, where we are called upon to shed our old identities and embrace new possibilities.

Embracing change requires us to surrender to the process of transformation, trusting in the inherent wisdom of life to guide us through the journey. It invites us to let go of attachments to the familiar and the comfortable, and to embrace the unknown with curiosity and courage.

Just as the butterfly emerges from the chrysalis with newfound strength and resilience, so too do we discover our capacity to adapt, evolve, and thrive amidst the uncertainties of life. By embracing change as an opportunity for growth and renewal, we unlock our full potential and spread our wings to explore new horizons.

In this way, the process of metamorphosis reminds us that change is not something to be feared or resisted, but celebrated as an essential aspect of the human experience. It is through embracing change that we discover the beauty of our own transformation, and the boundless potential that lies within each of us to flourish and thrive in times of transition.

Even in our childhood, we can liken ourselves to caterpillars, navigating the world with innocence and curiosity. Like caterpillars, children are constantly growing and learning, consuming knowledge and experiences as they explore their surroundings. This stage is characterized by rapid development and the laying of foundational skills and beliefs that will shape our future.

As we transition from childhood to adolescence and young adulthood, we enter a period of profound transformation, much like the caterpillar entering the chrysalis. This stage is marked by significant physical, emotional, and cognitive changes as we navigate the complexities of identity formation, independence, and self- discovery. Just as the caterpillar undergoes a period of growth and reorganization within the chrysalis, we too experience internal shifts as we grapple with societal expectations, peer relationships, and personal aspirations.

In adulthood, we emerge from the metaphorical chrysalis as fully formed individuals, equipped with the skills, knowledge, and experiences acquired throughout our journey. Like the butterfly spreading its wings for the first time, we embark on our life's journey with a sense of purpose and direction, empowered to pursue our passions and contribute to the world around us. This stage is characterized by personal and professional achievements, the establishment of meaningful relationships, and the pursuit of fulfillment and happiness.

As we progress through life, we inevitably encounter the final stage of old age, akin to the twilight years of the butterfly's lifespan. In old age, we reflect on the journey we have undertaken, cherishing the memories and experiences that have shaped us into the individuals we have become. Like the butterfly gracefully soaring through the skies, we embrace the wisdom and perspective that come with age, finding fulfillment in the relationships we have nurtured and the legacies we leave behind.

Through the metaphor of metamorphosis, we gain insight into the cyclical nature of human life, characterized by periods of growth, transformation, and renewal. By embracing each stage of the journey with courage, resilience, and gratitude, we can navigate life's transitions with grace and authenticity, ultimately discovering the beauty and meaning inherent in the human experience.

FINDING MEANING AND PURPOSE AMIDST TRANSITION IS IMPORTANT

Life transitions often challenge our sense of meaning and purpose, causing us to reassess our goals, values, and priorities. During times of change, it becomes crucial to cultivate a deeper understanding of what truly matters to us and how we can align our actions with our core values.

This is the process of finding meaning and purpose amidst transition by encouraging introspection and reflection. It involves asking profound questions about our identity, aspirations, and the legacy we wish to leave behind.

One aspect of this exploration involves reflecting on experiences and identifying patterns or themes that resonate deeply with us. By recognizing the moments when we felt most fulfilled or engaged, we can gain insight into the activities, relationships, or pursuits that hold significance for us.

Furthermore, this emphasizes the importance of embracing change as an opportunity for personal growth and self-discovery. Instead of viewing transition as a threat to our sense of purpose, we can reframe it as a catalyst for transformation and renewal. By remaining open to new possibilities and experiences, we can uncover hidden talents, passions, and sources of inspiration that enrich our lives.

Additionally, finding meaning and purpose amidst transition often involves connecting with something greater than ourselves. Whether through spirituality, community service, or creative expression, engaging in activities that foster a sense of connection and contribution can provide a profound sense of purpose and fulfillment.

TRANSFORMING FEAR INTO FUEL: EMBRACING CHANGE WITH COURAGE

This focuses on how we can harness the energy of fear that often accompanies change and use it as motivation to embrace transformation with courage and resilience.

Change inevitably brings uncertainty, and it's natural for fear to arise as we face the unknown. However, instead of allowing fear to paralyze us, we can learn to channel it into a source of strength and determination.

Firstly, this emphasizes the importance of acknowledging and accepting our fears. By recognizing and naming our fears, we can begin to understand their underlying causes and how they may be holding us back from embracing change. This self-awareness is the first step towards transforming fear into a catalyst for growth.

Next, it encourages individuals to reframe their perception of fear. Rather than viewing fear as a barrier to progress, we can see it as an indicator of the significance of the change we are facing. Fear often arises when we are stepping outside of our comfort zones and venturing into uncharted territory. By reframing fear as a natural response to growth and evolution, we can begin to see it as a sign that we are on the right path.

Moreover, this highlights the importance of cultivating courage in the face of fear. Courage is not the absence of fear, but rather the ability to take action in spite of it. It involves facing our fears head-on, acknowledging the risks involved, and moving forward with determination and resilience. By embracing courage as a guiding principle, we can navigate change with confidence and conviction, knowing that we have the inner strength to overcome any obstacles that may arise.

Finally, it emphasizes the transformative power of taking action in the face of fear. By stepping outside of our comfort zones and embracing change with courage, we open ourselves up to new possibilities and opportunities for growth. Each time we confront our fears and take a step forward, we build resilience and confidence, reinforcing our ability to navigate change with grace and resilience.

In essence, this encourages individuals to view fear not as a hindrance, but as a powerful catalyst for transformation. By embracing change with courage and resilience, we can navigate life's transitions with confidence and emerge stronger, wiser, and more empowered than ever before.

> ***"Embracing change is not merely about adapting to the winds of transformation, but about unfurling our sails and setting course for new horizons. In the storms of transition, we discover our true capacity to soar."***

From the smallest shifts in our daily routines to the profound transformations that shape our identities and aspirations, navigating change is an inherent part of the human experience. In the exploration of "Embracing Change: Thriving in Times of Transition," we have journeyed through the complexities of change, uncovering insights and strategies to navigate life's transitions with courage, resilience, and grace.

Through understanding the nature of change and the challenges it presents, we have learned to embrace uncertainty as an opportunity for growth rather than a barrier to progress. By cultivating resilience in the face of adversity and harnessing the power of adaptability, we have discovered our innate capacity to thrive amidst life's uncertainties.

Moreover, we have explored the importance of finding meaning and purpose amidst transition, anchoring ourselves in our core values and aspirations as guiding principles for navigating change.

Through building support networks and fostering connections with others, we have learned the importance of community and collaboration in times of transition.

Furthermore, we learnt, embracing change with courage and determination, knowing that each step forward brings us closer to realizing our full potential. By reframing our perception of fear and viewing it as a natural response to growth and evolution, we have unlocked the transformative power of taking action in spite of our fears.

May we approach change not as a threat to be feared, but as an opportunity to embrace the beauty and possibility inherent in the human experience. By navigating life's transitions with courage, resilience, and grace, may we emerge stronger, wiser, and more empowered than ever before, ready to embrace the ever-changing landscape of our lives with open hearts and minds.

19

EMBRACING THE UNKNOWN: THRIVING INUNCERTAINTY

In life, uncertainty looms as a constant companion, casting its shadow over our aspirations, plans, and dreams. In the face of the unknown, we are often confronted with a myriad of fears and doubts, grappling with the uncertainty of what lies ahead. However, amidst the ever-shifting landscape of uncertainty, there exists a profound opportunity—to not merely survive, but to thrive in the face of ambiguity and unpredictability.

From the depths of fear and anxiety to the heights of resilience and growth, we delve into the complexities of navigating uncertainty with courage, resilience, and grace.

"Embracing the Unknown: Thriving in Uncertainty" is a manifesto for living fully and authentically in the face of uncertainty. It is a testament to the resilience of the human spirit, the capacity for growth and adaptation, and the enduring power of hope and optimism.

Let's draw inspiration from the words of Steve Jobs, the visionary co-founder of Apple Inc, to explore the concept of embracing the unknown and thriving in uncertainty.

Steve Jobs once famously said, "Your work is going to fill a large part of your life, and the only way to be truly satisfied is to do what you believe is great work. And the only way to do great work is to love what you do. If you haven't found it yet, keep looking. Don't settle. As with all matters of the heart, you'll know when you find it."

Jobs' words encapsulate the essence of embracing the unknown with passion and purpose. Throughout his career, Jobs navigated numerous uncertainties and setbacks, from being ousted from Apple in the mid-1980s to facing the challenges of revolutionizing entire industries with groundbreaking products like the iPhone and iPad.

Despite the uncertainties he encountered, Jobs remained steadfast in his commitment to pursuing his vision and doing what he loved. He viewed challenges not as roadblocks, but as opportunities for innovation and growth. Instead of settling for mediocrity or complacency, Jobs embraced the unknown with a relentless drive to create something truly remarkable.

Moreover, Jobs' willingness to embrace uncertainty was rooted in his belief in the power of intuition and creativity. He famously trusted his gut instincts and encouraged others to do the same, often eschewing market research and conventional wisdom in favor of his own vision for the future. By embracing uncertainty and taking bold risks,

Jobs and his team at Apple revolutionized entire industries and transformed the way we interact with technology.

Furthermore, Jobs' journey serves as a testament to the transformative power of resilience and perseverance. Despite facing numerous setbacks and failures throughout his career, Jobs never lost sight of his passion and purpose. He viewed each obstacle as an opportunity to learn and grow, using adversity as fuel for innovation and creativity. In essence, Steve Jobs' life and legacy inspire us to embrace the unknown with passion, purpose, and resilience. By following his example and approaching life's uncertainties with a sense of curiosity, determination, and creativity, we can navigate the uncharted waters of existence with courage and grace, ultimately finding fulfillment and success in our endeavors.

> ***"Uncertainty is not the enemy of progress; it is the catalyst for innovation and growth. Embrace the unknown, and you'll discover endless opportunities waiting to be explored."***

One notable study conducted by researchers at University College London (UCL) investigated how the brain responds to uncertainty using fMRI. The study found that when participants were presented with uncertain situations, such as gambling tasks or decision-making scenarios with ambiguous outcomes, certain areas of the brain, including the prefrontal cortex and anterior cingulate cortex, showed increased activity.

These brain regions are involved in higher-order cognitive functions, such as decision-making, planning, and monitoring, suggesting that uncertainty triggers a cognitive response aimed at evaluating options and adapting behavior accordingly.

Furthermore, research in the field of neuroplasticity has shown that the brain has a remarkable ability to reorganize itself in response to new experiences and challenges. When confronted with uncertainty, the brain undergoes structural and functional changes that enable individuals to better cope with unpredictable situations and learn from their experiences.

By understanding how the brain responds to uncertainty and leveraging its inherent plasticity, individuals can cultivate resilience, creativity, and agility in the face of unpredictable circumstances, ultimately thriving in the midst of uncertainty.

THRIVING IN UNCERTAIN TIMES: CULTIVATING A GROWTH MINDSET FOR RESILIENCE AND ADAPTABILITY

In this we delve into the principles of cultivating a growth mindset as a means to thrive in uncertain times. A growth mindset, as coined by psychologist Carol Dweck, refers to the belief that abilities and intelligence can be developed through dedication and effort. This mindset contrasts with a fixed mindset, which assumes that abilities are innate and unchangeable.

During uncertain times, having a growth mindset is particularly valuable as it fosters resilience and adaptability. Instead of viewing challenges and setbacks as insurmountable obstacles, individuals with a growth mindset see them as opportunities for learning and growth.

One aspect of cultivating a growth mindset involves reframing failures and setbacks as valuable learning experiences. Rather than dwelling on mistakes or setbacks, individuals with a growth mindset approach them with curiosity and resilience, seeking to understand what went wrong and how they can improve in the future.

Furthermore, a growth mindset involves embracing the process of learning and development, rather than focusing solely on outcomes or achievements. By adopting a mindset of continuous improvement and growth, individuals are better equipped to navigate uncertainty and adapt to changing circumstances.

Moreover, cultivating a growth mindset involves fostering a sense of optimism and possibility, even in the face of uncertainty. By focusing on opportunities rather than limitations, individuals can maintain a sense of hope and resilience, even during challenging times.

Practical strategies for cultivating a growth mindset may include:

1. **Viewing effort as a path to mastery:** Understand that effort and perseverance are essential for achieving long-term goals.
2. **Learning from feedback:** Rather than being defensive or discouraged by criticism, see feedback as a valuable opportunity for growth and improvement.

3. **Cultivating resilience:** Develop coping mechanisms and strategies for bouncing back from setbacks and adversity.
4. **Fostering a sense of possibility:** Cultivate optimism and maintain a sense of hope, even in uncertain times.

Overall, cultivating a growth mindset is a powerful tool for thriving in uncertain times. By embracing challenges, learning from failures, and maintaining a sense of optimism and possibility, individuals can navigate uncertainty with resilience, adaptability, and confidence, ultimately thriving in the face of adversity.

> ***"Embracing uncertainty is not about predicting the future; it's about trusting yourself to navigate whatever comes your way with courage, creativity, and grace."***

It emphasizes that embracing uncertainty does not involve trying to foresee or control every outcome, but rather, it entails cultivating trust in oneself to navigate whatever challenges or opportunities arise with courage, creativity, and grace.

Firstly, it highlights the futility of trying to predict the future with certainty. The reality is that the future is inherently uncertain, and attempting to predict or control every possible outcome is often futile and anxiety-inducing. Instead of fixating on trying to foresee every twist and turn, embracing uncertainty involves accepting the unpredictability of life and being open to whatever may come.

Secondly, it underscores the importance of trusting oneself in the face of uncertainty. When navigating uncertain situations, it's essential to have confidence in one's abilities, intuition, and resilience. Trusting oneself means having faith in one's capacity to adapt, problem-solve, and make decisions, even in the absence of complete information or certainty.

Furthermore, it emphasizes the qualities of courage, creativity, and grace as essential attributes for navigating uncertainty. Courage is necessary for facing the unknown with resilience and determination, even when it feels daunting or uncomfortable. Creativity enables individuals to think outside the box, explore new possibilities, and adapt to changing circumstances creatively. Grace involves navigating uncertainty with a sense of poise, acceptance, and humility, even amidst challenges or setbacks.

To know more about the concept let's think about this book. "The Road Less Traveled" is a classic self-help book that explores the journey of personal growth and spiritual development. One of the central themes of the book is the idea that embracing uncertainty is essential for personal growth and fulfillment.

Peck argues that life is inherently uncertain and that embracing the unknown is necessary for progress and self-realization. He emphasizes the importance of facing our fears, confronting the uncertainties of life, and stepping outside of our comfort zones in order to grow and evolve as individuals.

Throughout the book, Peck shares insights and anecdotes from his own life and clinical practice to illustrate the transformative power of embracing uncertainty. He explores the idea that uncertainty is not something to be avoided or feared, but rather embraced as an essential aspect of the human experience.

Moreover, "The Road Less Traveled" emphasizes the importance of taking personal responsibility for our lives and choices, even in the face of uncertainty. Peck argues that by embracing uncertainty and taking ownership of our decisions, we can cultivate resilience, adaptability, and inner strength.

Additionally, the book encourages readers to cultivate a sense of curiosity and openness to the unknown. Peck suggests that by approaching uncertainty with a sense of curiosity and wonder, rather than anxiety or resistance, we can uncover hidden opportunities for growth and self-discovery.

"The Road Less Traveled" offers valuable insights into the importance of embracing uncertainty as a pathway to personal growth and fulfillment. Through Peck's wisdom and guidance, readers are reminded that uncertainty is not something to be avoided, but rather embraced as an essential aspect of the journey towards self-realization. By facing our fears, taking personal responsibility for our lives, and approaching uncertainty with curiosity and openness, we can navigate life's uncertainties with courage and grace, ultimately thriving in the face of adversity.

> ***Embracing challenges: Instead of avoiding difficulties, actively seek out opportunities to stretch and challenge yourself.***

"Embracing challenges" entails adopting a proactive approach towards difficulties rather than avoiding them altogether. Instead of shying away from situations that may be uncomfortable or daunting, this mindset encourages individuals to actively seek out opportunities that push them beyond their comfort zones.

By actively seeking out challenges, individuals expose themselves to new experiences and opportunities for growth. These challenges could manifest in various forms, such as tackling a new project at work, learning a new skill or hobby, or engaging in activities that require stepping outside of familiar routines.

The rationale behind this approach is that facing challenges head-on fosters personal development and resilience. When individuals confront obstacles and difficulties, they have the opportunity to test their limits, develop new skills, and build confidence in their ability to overcome adversity.

Moreover, actively seeking out challenges can lead to a sense of empowerment and accomplishment. By pushing oneself beyond perceived limitations and achieving success in the face of adversity, individuals strengthen their self-efficacy and belief in their ability to overcome future challenges.

Additionally, embracing challenges fosters a growth mindset – the belief that abilities and intelligence can be developed through dedication and effort. Rather than viewing challenges as threats to one's competence or self-worth, individuals with a growth mindset see them as opportunities for learning and improvement.

Through the wisdom of renowned personalities, scientific research, and timeless literature, we've learned that embracing uncertainty is not about predicting or controlling the future, but rather about trusting ourselves to navigate the unknown with courage, creativity, and grace. Whether through the teachings of "The Alchemist" or the insights of "The Road Less Traveled," we are reminded that the key to thriving in uncertain times lies in embracing the present moment and approaching each challenge with resilience and adaptability.

Ultimately, by embracing uncertainty as an inevitable part of the human experience and focusing on the richness of the present moment, we can unlock the potential for growth, self-discovery, and fulfillment. It is through this courageous embrace of the unknown that we can navigate life's uncertainties with grace and resilience, ultimately emerging stronger, wiser, and more fulfilled on the other side.